NEW DESIGN FOR OLD BUILDINGS

Roger Hunt
and Iain Boyd
Foreword by
Kevin McCloud

In association with the
Society for the Protection of
Ancient Buildings

RIBA ⊞ **Publishing**

© RIBA Publishing, 2017

Published by RIBA Publishing, part of RIBA Enterprises Ltd, The Old Post Office, St Nicholas Street, Newcastle upon Tyne, NE1 1RH

ISBN 978-1-85946-612-4

The rights of Roger Hunt and Iain Boyd to be identified as the Authors of this Work have been asserted in accordance with the Copyright, Designs and Patents Act 1988 sections 77 and 78.

British Library Cataloguing-in-Publication Data

A catalogue record for this book is available from the British Library.

Commissioning Editor: Elizabeth Webster
Design and production: Michèle Woodger
Printed and bound by W&G Baird, Great Britain
Cover design: Kneath Associates
Cover image: Royal William Yard, Plymouth – Gillespie Yunnie Architects / Urban Splash

While every effort has been made to check the accuracy and quality of the information given in this publication, neither the Authors nor the Publisher accept any responsibility for the subsequent use of this information, for any errors or omissions that it may contain, or for any misunderstandings arising from it.

The Society for the Protection of Ancient Buildings (SPAB) is a charitable company limited by guarantee registered in England and Wales. Company number 5743962. Charity number 1113753. Scottish charity number SCO39244.

www.ribaenterprises.com

CONTENTS

FOREWORD

This book skilfully deals with one of the horny nubs of architecture: how to work on and with old buildings in such a way that respects and reveres them, while also adding of our time, while *also* aiming for something yet greater – a dialogue between ancient and modern that lifts the value and meaning of both. In this it embodies the core values of the man whose writings were highly influential in the foundation of the conservation movement in nineteenth century Britain, John Ruskin, who wrote: *'Our duty is to preserve what the past has had to say for itself, and to say for ourselves what shall be true for the future.'*

It's an important point, well-made in this volume and worth repeating – nay, shouting from the shingle and sedum rooftops – that good conservation demands a clear and rigorous contemporary approach for new work just as much as it requires delicacy and respect in dealing with the past. We muddle the two at our peril because it leads to rootless, confusing and ineffectual architecture that does not speak of its time or value its own past.

Doing both these things well and clearly, however, is a mark of a civilised culture and we have come to recognise that those cities in which the historical fabric is conserved and celebrated alongside confident, contemporary architecture are places that score most highly for liveability. Making sense of the past, after all, helps us understand where we are and where we're going.

But physically joining up old and new is something else. If standalone new architecture is a complicated business, the process of designing new buildings to adapt and reinvent ancient ones is a fraught one. Roger and Iain bring a discerning critical eye to this finickity corner of architecture, one beset by the challenges and conditions of both contemporary building requirements and the onerous demands of dealing with protected, fragile and sometimes poorly built dangerous structures. In this book they skilfully guide us through the work of some of the best 21st century examples, their erudition underscored by a deep understanding of conservation theory and principles.

Importantly, they also bring an understanding of something less tangible. How, by reworking, refreshing and reimagining our built environment, we revitalise its stories – and therefore ourselves. We are narrative creatures who make sense of our world in our imaginations, assembling our own story from that of what is around us. This book shows how we can make that narrative clear, true and vital while adding to it with the energy and truth of our own time.

Kevin McCloud

ADVISORY NOTE

Please note that every building is different, and so designs, materials and suggestions examined in this book will not be relevant in every instance and should not be applied without careful thought. If you are in doubt, seek suitably experienced professional advice. This also relates to the photographs and illustrations, which may indicate an approach but should not be treated as a guarantee of a suitable course of action in every circumstance.

HISTORIC ENVIRONMENT CONSENTS

The UK has strict laws which protect historic buildings, areas, sites and landscapes, and it is in your interest to adhere to these. Before beginning any work of repair, alteration or development to a building, any structures within its grounds or the site on which it stands, it is essential to check with the local planning authority whether any consent will be needed. In the case of all listed buildings, remember that the interior as well as the exterior is protected and that the listing may extend to ancillary structures within the curtilage of the main building.

PREFACE

New design for old buildings must be seen as just one phase in a long timeline spanning decades, even centuries, and succeeds when the relationship between new and old is well understood and skilfully managed. Good design requires a deep understanding of what has gone before, as well as a vision of how the new and old parts will perform together long into the future. In this book, we have followed the SPAB principle that good new architecture can sit happily alongside old and is preferable to poor pastiche; our aim is to provide an insight into the factors and considerations that go towards making a successful scheme.

Many examples of new design in old buildings have been chronicled and celebrated in recent years, often featuring projects from North America and Europe. In this book, we focus solely on buildings from within the UK, and our research has revealed a rich supply of exemplary schemes, both large and small, as well as countless designers and craftspeople who demonstrate a thoughtful and creative approach. By its nature, it is not an exhaustive study, and there are many good projects which space has precluded us from mentioning.

Buildings result from collaborative effort and a creative vision shared between a number of people. Much of our focus is on the architects and designers who provide the vital narrative of imaginative thinking and execution. Architects understand that design is an overarching process that provides both a solution to an entire building brief and deals with more specific small-scale issues of detailing. We do not presume to set out in depth the processes of design nor the specifics of what design is.

We have attempted to present the best philosophical and practical thinking on the subject. The 'old' buildings featured in this book date from the medieval period to the second half of the twentieth century, where the same issues and problems are found. Rather than analysing a select few case studies, we have drawn from a larger sample and looked at more than one hundred buildings; some appearing once within the book, others numerous times. In some cases the element of new work we have chosen may stand out as exemplary over other less-informed work within the same scheme. A selection of featured buildings follows this preface.

Our readers, we hope, will extend beyond building professionals, to include students, homeowners and all those who care for old buildings and are faced with the challenges of adapting and using them in future decades. Above all, we aspire to encourage owners and architects to be braver and to understand that good new design is essential in ensuring the life and sustainability of old buildings.

Roger Hunt

Iain Boyd

FEATURED BUILDINGS

ALL SOULS BOLTON
GREATER MANCHESTER | 2014
OMI ARCHITECTS
In a socially deprived area of Bolton, the redundant church had lost any connection to its community. Inspired and driven by local voices from the business, leisure and faith sectors, an adaptable and multi-use building has been created through the insertion of a series of pods. It is now successfully used for office, community and social purposes.

ASTLEY CASTLE
NUNEATON, WARWICKSHIRE | 2012
WITHERFORD WATSON MANN
The historic fabric dates mainly from the 16th century and the building was in continuous occupation until a fire in 1978. Now converted into holiday accommodation by the Landmark Trust, the sense of ruination in the building is still strong, with some elements left open to the weather and the new work clearly readable.

BRACKEN HOUSE
FRIDAY STREET, LONDON | 1992
HOPKINS ARCHITECTS
Originally housing the Financial Times, Bracken House was destined for complete redevelopment but, in 1987, became the first post-Second World War building to be listed. The redundant printing works was stripped from the building's centre and, drawing on the form of an Italian palazzo, a new main entrance was created, flanked by the original wings.

BRITISH MUSEUM, WORLD CONSERVATION AND EXHIBITIONS CENTRE
BLOOMSBURY, LONDON | 2014
ROGERS STIRK HARBOUR + PARTNERS
Bringing all the museum's conservators under one roof for the first time, the WCEC provides 18,000 sq m space. With much of this accommodated underground, what is visible from the street belies the scale of the project and, slotted between existing wings of the Grade I listed museum, appears clean, modest and proportionate.

COPPER KINGDOM CENTRE
AMLWCH, NORTH WALES | 2014
DONALD INSALL ASSOCIATES
In the 18th century the port was the world's busiest for copper export with the copper ore stored in large quayside bins. The scheme has transformed these bins to create a visitor centre while embracing the challenge of forming a junction between the modern building and the bare, often wet, rock face. Appropriately, copper is the cladding material.

THE CROSS BATH
BATH, SOMERSET | 2006
DONALD INSALL ASSOCIATES
Two hundred years after its fashionable peak, the natural hot spring facilities in Bath were dilapidated and unusable. A council-initiated regeneration project with a commercial partner resulted in extensive research that revealed some of the earliest plans and the new cantilevered canopy and oval pool take their inspiration from these.

DITCHLING MUSEUM OF ART + CRAFT
DITCHLING, EAST SUSSEX | 2014
ADAM RICHARDS ARCHITECTS
Housing a nationally important collection of items connected to Eric Gill and his group, the museum occupies the former school on the village green. The new scheme radically changed the layout and orientation of what was there before but represents a carefully considered development that takes elements of colour and design from Gill's work.

DOVECOTE STUDIO, SNAPE MALTINGS
SAXMUNDHAM, SUFFOLK | 2009
HAWORTH TOMPKINS
Set within Snape Maltings, the rehearsal and concert venue created by Benjamin Britten in the 1960s from former warehouse and industrial buildings, the studio is used by artists and writers. It occupies the ruin of a former 19th century dovecot and was formed through the insertion of a one piece welded steel structure that echoes the building's original form.

FEERINGBURY BARN
FEERING, ESSEX | 2011
HUDSON ARCHITECTS
A barn conversion which imaginatively addressed one of the main problems when undertaking such projects: the challenge of introducing light without creating unsympathetic openings to the walls or roof. The result provides both a restrained appearance from the outside and the opportunity to fully appreciate the structure of the barn from within.

GARDEN MUSEUM
LAMBETH, LONDON | 2008, 2017
DOW JONES ARCHITECTS
Standing next to Lambeth Palace, the church of St Mary-at-Lambeth was threatened by demolition in the 1970s. It was rescued by the founding of the Garden Museum on the site. The building was poorly suited for such use but spaces needed for meetings, exhibitions and other facilities have been created through new work woven within the fabric of the former church.

GASWORKS
LOWER SLAUGHTER, GLOUCESTERSHIRE | 2014
CHRIS DYSON ARCHITECTS
Originally a 19th century stone cottage, the need for extra space was jointly addressed by the client and the architect with significant input from the local conservation officer. The resulting range of extensions in Cor-Ten steel echo agricultural vernacular materials and forms while reimagining the carbide gas cylinder formerly on the site.

THE GRANARY
BARKING AND DAGENHAM, LONDON | 2011
POLLARD THOMAS EDWARDS
Many earlier alterations and additions were removed from the original building while a sympathetic twin was created alongside. This strikes a balance between echoing some aspects of its older neighbour and taking an entirely new direction in terms of form and materials, at the same time serving as a focal point for the regeneration of the entire area.

GUNPOWDER MILL
WALTHAM ABBEY, ESSEX | 2009
POLLARD THOMAS EDWARDS

From the 18th century until the early 1990s, the Royal Gunpowder Mills was a production and research centre for explosives. The subsequent conversion into office space saw a modern extension to one side with the original mill's internal volume broken up by a series of interconnected platforms, stairs and balconies referencing its industrial past.

HOLBURNE MUSEUM
BATH, SOMERSET | 2011
ERIC PARRY ARCHITECTS

Opened as a hotel in 1796, the building was remodelled in the early 20th century to house the Holburne collection, but the facilities were inadequate and the connection to the landscape at the rear poor. The extension, notable for its use of glass cladding and faience fins, remedies these problems, providing both museum and café space.

HOLY TRINITY CHURCH
GOODRAMGATE, YORK | 2010
SIMMONSHERRIFF LLP

Many churches seek to introduce kitchen and toilet facilities for their buildings, often with disabled access also in mind. At Holy Trinity this has been achieved in a very restricted space through a modest extension which has been constructed using a thoughtful range of materials and finishes, including oak cladding fashioned with an adze to provide texture.

HUNSETT MILL
STALHAM, NORFOLK | 2010
ACME

Until 1900 the cottage was home to the keeper of a windmill that pumped water on the Norfolk Broads. Both the cottage and the surrounding site have been rationalised to reveal their simplicity. Although large, the building that forms the modern extension avoids being the main focus, with the dominant fenestration reflecting the open skies and landscape.

KEW PALACE
RICHMOND, SURREY | 2007
PURCELL

Kew Palace, built in 1631 and the former home of George III, is in the care of Historic Royal Palaces. Many parts were inaccessible to the public and the greatest challenge was to introduce a lift. The choice of site and the form of the external lift shaft was based on historic precedent – a former water closet shaft – and represents the least intrusive solution.

LSO ST LUKE'S
OLD STREET, LONDON | 2000
LEVITT BERNSTEIN

Subsidence and the necessary removal of the roof in the 1950s left St Luke's a virtual ruin until the London Symphony Orchestra took on the building to turn it into a rehearsal and concert venue. As well as conserving the building's historic fabric, the scheme faced and met a range of challenges, notably acoustic treatment to prevent sound transmission from the busy road outside.

MAGDALEN COLLEGE LONGWALL LIBRARY
OXFORD, OXFORDSHIRE | 2016
WRIGHT & WRIGHT ARCHITECTS

The Gothic Revival library was built in the mid-19th century and underwent an unsympathetic remodelling by Giles Gilbert Scott in the 1930s. The new work improved access to the whole of the Longwall quad, while a free-standing, timber-clad steel structure was inserted within the library, revealing the windows to their full height.

MARTELLO TOWER Y
BAWDSEY, SUFFOLK | 2010
PIERCY&COMPANY ARCHITECTS

During the Napoleonic Wars, 103 Martello towers were built along the British coast, this one in 1808. Unused and derelict, permission was given for conversion to a private residence. Challenges included its 3m thick walls, its Scheduled Ancient Monument status and its setting in an Area of Outstanding Natural Beauty and Site of Special Scientific Interest.

NATIONAL THEATRE
SOUTH BANK, LONDON | 2015
HAWORTH TOMPKINS

The regeneration of the theatre highlights issues relating to conserving 20th-century buildings. Aspects were returned to Denys Lasdun's original 1960s designs, others remodelled to meet current and future needs. Adding a production workshop provided much-needed facilities, as well as public access for educational and viewing purposes.

PIER ARTS CENTRE
STROMNESS, ORKNEY | 2007
REIACH AND HALL ARCHITECTS

Among the warehouses, stone buildings and boat sheds, the Pier Arts Centre brings a recognisable form to the quay at Stromness through a mixture of refurbishment and new works. At the same time, with its facade that shifts from solid to void, it presents something that is entirely new through its material composition and aesthetic form.

POD GALLERY
SOUTH GLOUCESTERSHIRE | 2015
STONEWOOD DESIGN

The owners' brief was to take the substantial and listed agricultural barn adjoining their house and create a space and atmosphere suitable for an art gallery. The solution saw the insertion of a freestanding pod that lines the volume of the barn. The cantilevered design has little or no impact on the historic fabric of the building while appearing to float in space.

RAMBLERS
PULBOROUGH, WEST SUSSEX | 2007
MOLE ARCHITECTS

The project involved the replacement of a 1960s addition with an extension visually separated from the original building by a frameless glass slot and clad externally in oak and clay tiles. Openings are formed from frameless glazing and are shuttered. While the new structure clearly contrasts with the old, there is a visual rhythm between the two.

ROYAL ACADEMY SACKLER GALLERIES
PICCADILLY, LONDON | 1991
JULIAN HARRAP WITH FOSTER + PARTNERS
Replacing the Diploma Galleries of 1869 above Burlington House, the Sackler Galleries deliver ideal environmental standards for exhibitions. The intervention exploits an existing light well between the Palladian original and the large Victorian gallery block to the north, so three eras of architecture and materials are now clearly visible.

SOUTHWARK CATHEDRAL
LAMBETH, LONDON | 2000
RICHARD GRIFFITHS ARCHITECTS
Added to the north of the cathedral, a two-storey wing contains a refectory on the ground floor and a function room/library on the first floor, while a linking building contains meeting rooms and a shop. A significant accessible entrance for the cathedral was created from the Thames footpath via a courtyard that evokes the site's former monastic cloisters.

ST ANDREW'S CHURCH
BRIDGE SOLLARS, HEREFORDSHIRE | 2010
COMMUNION ARCHITECTS
Used occasionally for services, the church is mostly given over to community use. The modest conversion of the 12th-century building has provided a warm, usable space for events. Involving minimum intervention, the scheme conceals a kitchen, toilet and services within a wooden pod that folds out when needed.

TANNERS HILL
DEPTFORD, LONDON | 2012
DOW JONES ARCHITECTS
This project involved a house in Deptford dating from the 17th century and rebuilt or recast around 1750. The scheme has created both a modern home and space for occasional use as an art gallery, with an internal courtyard that allows in plentiful natural light. The building's history and earlier finishes are revealed to great effect and no attempt is made to disguise the progress of its development over time.

THE WAPPING HOUSE
WAPPING, LONDON | 2014
CHRIS DYSON ARCHITECTS
Replacing an earlier addition, the two-storey extension is a modern and subtle updating of Georgian styling. Details are echoed and the overall appearance is of complementary tones and materials but there is an unashamed simplification of form at every level with, for example, bronze casements rather than sashes occupying the window openings.

THE WHITE HOUSE
ISLE OF COLL, INNER HEBRIDES | 2010
WT ARCHITECTURE
With historical connections to James Boswell and to Samuel Johnson who toured the Hebrides and stayed in 1773, the house had fallen into ruin, with a distinctive cleft through one of the gable walls. The structure was sensitively consolidated and repaired, and an addition was constructed, while maintaining an appearance of semi-ruination from a distance.

INTRODUCTION

FIGURE 0.00
Staircase inserted at the Snape Maltings concert venue (left)

FIGURE 0.01
William Morris, co-founder of the SPAB (right).

The Society for the Protection of Ancient Buildings was founded by William Morris and Philip Webb in 1877 and is the oldest and most technically expert organisation fighting to save old buildings from decay, demolition and damage. Few, if any, other bodies have considered in such depth, or over such a length of time, the relationship between conservation methods and the visual effect of new design when applied to buildings and sites in the historic environment. As a conservation body, it is often assumed that the SPAB prefers new work to be 'in keeping' and matched to older fabric, whereas the opposite is true: the Society would rather see architecture that is clearly of its time and readable as such – a philosophy which is embedded in the Society's ethos.

THE SPAB MANIFESTO

On the founding of the SPAB, William Morris and other founder members published a manifesto with an emphasis on honesty to fabric and respect for layers of history. It set out the Society's distinctive philosophy of conservative repair and campaigned for the sensitive care of old buildings using traditional materials and skills.

Although produced in response to the conservation problems of the nineteenth century, when churches in particular were the subject of speculative 'restoration', the Manifesto extends protection to buildings of 'all times and styles' and remains to this day the philosophical basis for the Society's work. An early case that gathered support for the SPAB approach was the Cathedral and Abbey Church of Saint Alban in Hertfordshire. The abbey's layout dates from the eleventh century and the crossing tower from that period still stands. The following centuries included the dissolution of the monasteries, and years in which the building was subject to natural decay interspersed with rounds of fundraising for repairs and new works. Nevertheless, it arrived at the middle of the nineteenth century still standing and bearing witness to eight centuries of change.

At this point it came to the attention of prominent Victorian architects who sought to 'reimagine' churches in England, scraping away the accumulations of history and imposing an expression of what was felt to be the true spirit of an English Catholic style. This enthusiasm went with a kind of counter-factual vision, as if the Reformation had never happened. With the wealth then available, these changes could be extensive and radical.

Sir George Gilbert Scott began a programme of 'backdating improvements' at St Albans but it was the work there of Sir Edmund Beckett, later Lord Grimthorpe, that chiefly concerned Morris and galvanised the SPAB in its campaigning that became known as 'anti-scrape'. Grimthorpe did not lack funds, but he was largely untrained, autocratic and extremely ambitious. As a result, his legacy is a far cry from the best Victorian Gothic work exemplified by AWN Pugin and members of the Scott family. Unsympathetic to the building, it saw the obliteration of large sections of the abbey in the 1880s, including the entire west front, which was replaced with an entirely speculative neo-Gothic elevation.

The words and spirit of Morris's original Manifesto still inform the choices and actions of professionals and craftspeople both in the UK and abroad, and have provided concepts for the main international conservation charters. Since 1877, the Manifesto has been reinterpreted for the times on several occasions. The latest iteration is titled the 'SPAB Approach' and represents the Society's core values, outlining how the philosophical position is applied today. The SPAB thinking in these documents offers guidance rather than a set of rules – debate and dialogue are never precluded – and this book continues that tradition, linking the values to practical considerations of design and materials.

Figure 0.02
A rare 1870's photo of the 15th-century Wheathampstead window in the west front of St Albans Cathedral (far left).

Figure 0.03
St Albans Cathedral today after rebuilding by Lord Grimthorpe in the 1880s (left).

APPLICATION OF PHILOSOPHY

Despite the issue of new design for old buildings being beyond the original scope of the SPAB Manifesto, it very soon became relevant. The revolutionary (at the time) SPAB philosophy sought to consider the interests of a building in its future while valuing its past – concepts we would now recognise in terms of sustainability and managed change. Generally, modest, sympathetic works have always been acceptable to the SPAB – they allow continuing life for a building and contribute positively to its interest and story.

Somewhat controversially, the Manifesto also advocates that 'if it [an ancient structure] has become inconvenient for its present use ... raise another building rather than alter or enlarge the old one'. While this principle is not often pursued by today's SPAB, it was followed in the late nineteenth century at St Petrock's Church, Parracombe, in Devon, where it was felt that the building was too special to be radically altered and so a new church was constructed in the village while leaving the old one largely untouched.

Simple and vernacular but rich in character and craftsmanship, St Petrock's dates from the thirteenth century and, now Grade I listed, is in the care of the Churches Conservation Trust. This church was of the kind that the SPAB's founder members most appreciated – unspoilt and reeking of history. It is said to have been the last church in the area to have a band of musicians, and one pew still has a section cut out to accommodate a viola player's bow.

When, in September 1877, the rector of St Petrock's, the Rev PN Leakey, applied for membership of the SPAB, he wrote: *'I was glad to find that the last clause of your circular [the Manifesto] tallies precisely with what I am doing here viz; building a new church in order to avoid the necessity of destroying a very old one – but to carry this out I have had to combat much opposition.'*

This approach may not be practical or appropriate in every case, but it does remain arguable for the most special buildings that would be irrevocably harmed by significant change. In the SPAB Manifesto, Morris set out a philosophy that building works should be clearly readable and of their time. This was in response to destructive restoration and the fake turning back of time. The SPAB's philosophically rigorous approach puts the fabric of the building first, within the context of a value system based on conservative repair methods and the need to retain those qualities of age acquired over time.

Readability

The importance of understanding the layers of history in a building and a desire to make interventions legible is core to the SPAB's philosophy and many cases during its existence have challenged and sharpened thinking on the subject. Throughout this book, examples are featured which have successfully delivered new work which is sympathetic yet clearly differentiated from old.

The early case of the parish church of St Mary's Priory Church, at Deerhurst, near Tewkesbury, Gloucestershire, illustrates the pitfalls of ill-conceived new work. The Saxon apse had been largely destroyed in the seventeenth century and only a fragment remained. In August 1913 a proposal was put forward to rebuild the apse and the architect Harold Brakspear was appointed. Rebuilding the apse of a Saxon church was, understandably, something the SPAB did not take lightly, but Brakspear assured the Society that 'in the new work no attempt shall be made to imitate the fragment of the original apse which remains'.

When the drawings were supplied, the Society's view and that of the architect about a 'straightforward manner' of new building for the apse, proved to be far apart, and the Society felt that Saxon pastiche was being attempted. Brakspear continued to protest but by the time the SPAB's 1915 Annual Report was published it was noted that the scheme had been successfully opposed. Today the east end of St Mary's remains much as it was prior to the proposed scheme.

The layers of history, for example additions to a church, sometimes blend in over the centuries; even at a significant and much-visited site such as Hampton Court Palace in Surrey, the junction between Tudor and Stuart phases escapes the notice of most visitors.

Where there is a change of use, new works are often more visible. In Georgian and Victorian times and into the twentieth century, a number of insertions were made into nationally important ruins, which would be unthinkable now. However, due to their rarity and the thought and quality involved in the work, these are now appreciated as part of the peculiar evolutions of these buildings. Edwin Lutyens' renovation of Lindisfarne Castle is one example while, some 400 miles to the south, the ruined gatehouse of Newport Castle in Pembrokeshire was interleaved with a Victorian residence by the Lloyd family in 1859.

In Suffolk, Bury St Edmunds Abbey was founded in the tenth century but was largely reduced to ruins through collapse and fire by the fifteenth century and became a quarry for other buildings. In the

Figure 0.04
The largely untouched interior of St Petrock's Church, Devon (right).

Figure 0.05
The new brickwork at Astley Castle, Warwickshire, is sympathetic to the old in both the choice of material and its positioning in relation to the original wall line (far right).

eighteenth and nineteenth centuries, insertions were made in the outer abbey wall to create houses. There has been longstanding debate as to whether these post-medieval additions should be removed and the site returned to some previous point in its history. The difficulty of arguing for any particular date immediately presents itself and the SPAB would certainly argue against any attempt to turn back the clock for sentimental reasons of restoration or of supposed academic 'correctness'. Readability, and the avoidance of restoration or pastiche, continues to be a primary concern to the SPAB in the matter of new design, for the benefit of this and future generations.

New design

To prevent confusion, new work should express modern needs in a modern language and add to, rather than detract from, the building's historic provenance. This requires an explicit understanding of what is important and interesting about the old building and, in the case of a listed building, why it is listed.

The SPAB does not encourage attempts to recreate the past through interventions and does not support the construction of new buildings in imitation of the style of past eras. In the SPAB's view, to do so makes no more sense than to create paintings in the style of Delacroix or to attempt to write music in the same way as Bach. Cultural creations are of their time and responses must be relevant to their own century rather

Figure 0.06
Brakspear's neo-Saxon apse, proposed for St Mary's Priory Church, Gloucestershire, was rejected by the SPAB as pastiche.

SOUTH ELEVATION

Figure 0.07
Evolution of form and materials at Bury St Edmunds Abbey.

than the Renaissance, the French Revolution or the Baroque. Good design is integral to the SPAB's philosophy and is embraced in the principles that underwrite its conservation practices. For example, its approach to repair relies on integration but may see the use of complementary materials and techniques as part of the conservation work. Design should, in other words, be based on sympathy with subtle differences rather than following rigidly a specific architectural style or favouring any particular approach or material type.

Underlying this is the thought that new work should express modern needs in a modern language that is complementary to what exists. These are the only terms in which new can relate to old in a way which is positive and responsive at the same time. If an addition proves essential, it should not be made to outdo or outlast the original. The work of architect Philip Webb, and others close to the SPAB, demonstrates an endorsement of well-conceived new design and construction when adding to an old building. Webb placed great emphasis on the understanding of materials and used them skilfully to make his additions distinct but harmonious. Today, good new design is encouraged by the SPAB through its Philip Webb Award. The award encourages and celebrates the sympathetic re-use of existing buildings and sensitive new design in a historic context. It is an opportunity for students and architects in the early stages of their careers to demonstrate their design flair, their grasp of repair techniques and their engagement with the SPAB's principle of fitting the new to the old.

THE INFLUENCE OF WEBB

Often considered the father of Arts and Crafts architecture, Philip Webb worked with the grain of old buildings while drawing heavily on historical influences, and was prepared to enlarge an old house in addition to repairing it, in order to make it more habitable and extend its useful life. In doing this, he responded to and focused on the form of the existing structure while reacting to the design and fabric with which he was presented. Webb's designs consequently grew naturally out of the historic structure but, importantly, the references he makes to the past always have his own stamp. Where he introduces a window with heavy glazing bars, for example, it may have a flavour of the early eighteenth century but always with his own carefully considered – and often idiosyncratic – detailing included as well.

Webb's best known work is Standen House in West Sussex, which was completed in 1894. Deliberately informal and influenced by the vernacular, the house blends materials from the surrounding Weald – stone from the site, local brick, oak weatherboarding, tile-hanging and lime render – and is among the finest examples of Arts and Crafts workmanship. The land on which Standen now stands was originally made up of three farms: Stone, Hollybush and Standen. Early proposals had involved total demolition of these farms but, with great creativity and sympathy to the beauty of the site, Webb persuaded his clients to incorporate the existing historic buildings, including the threshing barn, Hollybush Farmhouse and the granary, into his design while creating a thoroughly modern home, complete with central heating and electricity.

PRACTICE AND CASEWORK

Today, the Society has a formal role as advisor to councils on listed building applications involving demolition. The SPAB's prinicples are upheld by its staff, volunteers and professional members, most visibly by its elected committee of Guardians who review some of the UK's most controversial planning proposals. Thousands of buildings survive that would have been lost, mutilated or badly repaired without the SPAB's advice or intervention. Many of the most famous structures in Britain are cared for by some of the several thousand people who have received the Society's training.

In practice, the application of these sound principles of conservation can still lead to remarkable, creative results. This was the case with the interior of the Great Dining Room at St Giles House, Wimborne St Giles, Dorset, which dates from the 1740s. Here, large portions of decorative plasterwork and panelling had been destroyed during dry rot treatment in the 1980s, with further elements dismantled and set aside.

During work by Philip Hughes Associates to bring the house back into use some 30 years later, it was decided to reinstate all of the dismantled original sections of the room. The work also involved the repair and conservation of the existing fabric, as well as fire protection and the introduction of services, but there was no attempt to restore missing areas of the plaster or wall linings where they had been lost.

Figure 0.09
Philip Webb's interpretation of a Queen Anne window at Standen.

Figure 0.10
The Great Dining Room at
St Giles House, Dorset,
after conservative repair.

There were several reasons for adopting this approach. The building fabric previously concealed behind the panelling demonstrates the complex historical development of this part of the house. Additionally, the form of the panelling's construction and wall linings is exposed where sections have been removed and is of great interest. None of this would be apparent if the missing decorative plaster and panelling were reinstated.

Surviving elements were re-fixed in their original locations. Reinstating only original fabric and leaving areas where it was missing means that everything that is present is authentic. It is also possible that other original fragments of the plaster or panelling may be discovered and the approach adopted does not preclude future reinstatement of missing elements.

The SPAB responds formally to the national planning casework load, often providing much-welcomed support to conservation officers. But while most development is planned, every year there are dramatic or major cases where the SPAB's principles are tested against not only its own archive of precedent but also prevailing public opinion. These situations illustrate how each case needs to be judged on its merits and practicality as well as underlying conservation philosophy.

Following the devastating fire in 1989 at Uppark, a National Trust property in South Harting, West Sussex, the then SPAB secretary, Philip Venning wrote: '*Where the destruction is total (for example in the area of the stairs) serious consideration should be given to employing the very best architects and designers of our day to add their contribution to the continuing history of the building. In years to come this should make Uppark far more alive and interesting than a sterile copy of a vanished work of art. There is no reason why today's designers should not create something of great beauty that complements what survives of the Georgian interior.'*

Subsequently the house was 'restored', the decision justified by the National Trust in part by the fact that most of the contents had survived and a detailed photographic record of the interior existed. Another regrettable contributory factor was said to be that the insurance cover would only permit a facsimile reconstruction.

Similarly, the SPAB supported new design alongside conservation after the 1993 IRA bomb damage to St Ethelburga's Church, Bishopsgate, London, one of the few medieval City churches to have survived the Great Fire of London. Again, a full reconstruction was the eventual course of action.

More recently, fires at the Glasgow School of Art (in 2014) and Clandon House in Surrey (in 2015) have again raised these questions. At Clandon, the National Trust is, at the time of writing, planning careful reinstatement of significant historic rooms with the re-imagining of other spaces on the upper floors.

In the case of the Glasgow School of Art, it has been concluded by many professionals and the public alike that reinstatement of the original Charles Rennie Mackintosh scheme is both desirable and possible. Up until the fire, the building existed more or less as designed and was extremely well documented. Restoration, it is argued, would not therefore be speculative. Despite this, questions and problems remain as to whether it can and should be an exact replica, faults and all. There is a view that, as the SPAB argued at Uppark, localised reinstatement to partially damaged fabric, complemented by sensitive new design where there was complete loss, might be appropriate, for example in the Glasgow School of Art's library. The work of a skilled craftsman-designer working in the Arts and Crafts tradition might act as a fitting substitute for, and a memorial to, the lost Mackintosh original.

The desire for reinstatement and a call for rebuilding is often the first reaction in the case of disaster, and in some cases there may be over-riding considerations to do with cultural or social identity which argue in favour of reconstruction.

But the default response should not be to assume that re-establishing the past through identical rebuilding is either the right thing to do or the wisest long-term solution. Reconstructions can never entirely recapture what has been lost and, at worst, can result in the deletion of history and allow for cultural amnesia.

BISHOPSGATE

Figure 0.11
Unbuilt proposal for St Ethelburga's Church, London, by Ettwein Bridges Architects.

After air-raid strikes on the Houses of Parliament in 1941, Sir Winston Churchill, the prime minister, insisted that the bomb-damaged archway from the Members' Lobby into the Commons Chamber be retained as a reminder for future generations, a move that was opposed at the time but which is now accepted as far-sighted wisdom.

The SPAB continues to press the case for conservative repair and the retention of historic fabric in old buildings, protecting their special qualities, peculiarities and atmosphere. At the same time it is vital to convey how useful, practical and relevant the Society's principles are in the creation of new design for old buildings.

Figure 0.12
Thermae Bath Spa
scheme in Bath (right)

CHAPTER 1:
EMBRACING GOOD DESIGN

Much is at stake when working with old buildings. Once lost, fabric, history and character can never be replaced and, if there is a failure to respect the old, the overall design solution is unlikely to be satisfactory. Introducing good design in the historic context relies on understanding, respect, good manners and skill.

Good design is perceived, not defined. While appreciation of architectural quality is in the eye of the beholder, the origins of good design are deep, complex and subtle, particularly when related to the historic environment. There is no 'one size fits all' solution and it is dangerous and presumptive to prescribe a formula. But there are powerful and understood ingredients that feed dynamic, contextual and ultimately successful projects when steered by an experienced hand.

The historic built environment is frequently composed of an amalgam of accretions, eclectic styles, mixed and matched materials, varying roof lines and irregular forms that come together to create a wonderful and harmonious whole, softened by the passage of time. Contributing to this is the inevitably transformative process that results from change of use and adaptation to meet the needs of succeeding owners and occupiers. This allows buildings to live on.

Many architects would rather start with a blank canvas, a scheme where they can express their ideas and creativity, and apply the experience of their long training. In reality, the vast majority of architects spend much of their time working with existing buildings, adapting and reinventing them through intervention and extension.

Figure 1.00
Glass-and-steel staircase at the Royal Academy of Arts' Sackler Galleries (left).

Figure 1.01
The 19th-century Granary, Barking, with a bronze-clad extension completed in 2011 (right).

The best and most successful examples retain the building's integrity and give new life to its essential parts. Design does not stand alone; conservation and sustainability are the other vital elements that form the triumvirate of disciplines that come into play when working with old buildings. New work that is added should neither confuse the expert nor offend the casual observer. It should be possible to understand what has happened to a building over time and, when viewed, the form and detail of alterations or additions should seem both clear and harmonious.

'If you can grasp the essence of the building you're approaching, then you have a basic framework from which to build a scheme of architectural design.'

Julian Harrap, Harrap Architects

THE NATURE OF DESIGN

William Morris enjoined his clients to '*have nothing in your house that you do not know to be useful or believe to be beautiful*'. What constitutes beauty and, by inference, good design is subjective. Writing in 1624 in *The Elements of Architecture*, Sir Henry Wotton interpreted the words of the first century BC Roman architect Vitruvius: '*In Architecture, as in all other operative arts, the end must direct the operation. The end is to build well. Well building hath three conditions – commodity, firmness and delight.*'

These simple words embrace both pitfalls and potential when making additions or alterations. Seeing the various phases of a building's evolution over time is appealing and instructive. Central to the idea of readability is that new work should be of today and reflect the very best that can be achieved in terms of materials, quality and design. This approach speaks of truth and honesty rather than seeking to mimic the past – something which is often referred to derogatorily as 'pastiche'.

Pastiche is a frequently used but misunderstood word in architecture, particularly when working in the historic environment. Many architectural styles that are now highly regarded have evolved through imitation, but attempting to blatantly copy or create a pastiche of an earlier age is rarely successful and there are nearly always some concessions to modernity in the detailing and materials.

Figure 1.02
Red House, Kent, designed by Philip Webb for William Morris in 1859.

More correctly, the words 'poor pastiche' better interpret our meaning when describing the poorly detailed, superficial and badly executed facsimiles of past architectural styles that are often seen today, both in new-build work and extensions to old buildings.

Often the term is applied to the 'identikit' method of styling which sees the random application of historic elements to the exteriors and interiors of buildings in an attempt to invoke the past. These include cornices and string courses that have little regard for craftsmanship, proportion or historic precedent. One of the most commonly seen offenders is the 'slipped' fanlight, where a traditionally separate architectural element (the fanlight: a fan-shaped glazed opening above the door, infilling the structural arch and providing light to the hallway) becomes instead an integral part of the front door. This represents an inept version of the original, typically Georgian, feature.

Such approaches respond to a view that new building work in historic settings should seek to replicate and match the appearance of existing structures. Skilfully done, 'good pastiche' may be appropriate in certain circumstances – for example, where part of a larger architectural composition has been lost – but, in general, new work should complement rather than slavishly imitate the old. New buildings do not need to look old nor ape the past in order to create a harmonious relationship with their historic surroundings and allow the primacy of older buildings to be clear.

Writing in 1892, Hugh Thackeray Turner, the SPAB's first secretary, noted that *'new parts should be as plain and unostentatious, though as sound and good, as possible and should clearly tell their own tale of having been erected in the nineteenth century, to harmonise with, but not to imitate, the earlier work'*.

> 'One seeks not to impose on a building, but to help it grow as it wants to. That isn't pastiche – pastiche is very often about imposing a preconceived set of ideas.'

Sir Donald Insall,
Donald Insall Associates

Figure 1.03
Compton Verney, Warwickshire, with a contrasting wing in stone added in 2004.

Figure 1.04
Modern and Victorian
gables at Gorton
Monastery, Manchester.

A twenty-first century example of this
thinking is the work carried out at
Compton Verney in Warwickshire by
Stanton Williams alongside conservation
architects Rodney Melville + Partners.
The transformation of the Grade I listed
mansion into a major arts venue included
the construction of environmentally
controlled galleries within the house and
a new education centre and offices set
among renovated historic outbuildings,
the new extension acting as a foil to the
existing house.

Figure 1.05
The barrel-roofed
extension at Binham
Priory, Norfolk.

The success of such additions results from the fact that they consider the use of the building over the
longer term rather than being a response to a short-term need. Carefully executed modern design suggests
honesty in execution and confidence in the architecture of today while adding a fresh layer of history to be
valued by future generations.

Good manners

'Well-mannered' is the description best suited to new design that succeeds in a historic context with
alterations and additions made in a form sympathetic and complementary to that which exists. These
schemes have seen new work fitted to old, rather than requiring that the old be adapted to fit the new. The
new structures do not compete unduly with the old building in form or position, but equally do not ape the
original or pretend to be historic; instead they fulfil modern needs in a modern style. Put simply, while not
necessarily 'quiet', they are mannerly rather than 'rude'.

Exemplifying the well-mannered approach is the work by Donald Insall Associates at Binham Priory in Norfolk, founded in the eleventh century. This project, completed in 1990, saw the creation of a new porch providing level access into the church for people with disabilities. Adjacent WCs for visitors to the priory ruins are within a self-effacing barrel-roofed extension, inserted on the site of the ruined north aisle of the historic building. This structure is kept deliberately low to avoid obscuring the sight lines through the windows from within the church and is undoubtedly modern in its design, despite the use of flint and stone to blend new with old.

Much bolder, but still mannerly, is the work undertaken to revive the Grade II* listed Gorton Monastery (the Church and Friary of St Francis) in east Manchester. Built between 1863 and 1872 and designed by Edward Pugin, son of AWN Pugin, the building suffered the indignity of appearing on the World Monument Fund Watch List of 100 Most Endangered Sites after it was vacated by the Franciscan order in 1989.

'If one goes from the starting point not of what architects and conservationists normally do, but what a designer working in the built environment should now be aware of, that designer would find themselves being both a creative artist and highly sensitive to and respectful of the existing structures around them. You'd end up with somebody who was both a conservationist and a creative designer and you'd find it very hard to draw a line between the two.'

Paddy Dillon, Haworth Tompkins

A major campaign to save the monastery and give it new life resulted in a scheme by Austin-Smith:Lord, completed in 2007. This included extensions and rebuilt sections which acknowledged the overall plan and form without fighting the High Victorian Gothic architecture. The building is now functional, popular and an inspiring venue for corporate, social and cultural events.

Figure 1.06
The Investcorp Building at St Antony's College, Oxford, abuts its neighbour (right).

Figure 1.07
A London warehouse loading door tells a story from function to redundancy (far right).

One building that arguably falls into the 'rude' category is the Investcorp Building for St Antony's College, Oxford, designed by Zaha Hadid Architects and completed in 2015. While the design is brilliant, innovative and makes good use of modern materials, the junctions with the older buildings appear ill-considered and ignore their forms.

THE DESIRE TO RETAIN THE OLD

Old buildings and the history and character they embody engender colossal interest and support both among building professions and the public. The past understandably conjures up nostalgia, romance and fantasy. Peeling paint, the broken window and the shabby doorcase of the urban terrace are potentially just as evocative as the ivy-clad ruin standing forlornly in the mist. As life becomes increasingly virtual, architecture's capacity to curate meaningful, physical experiences that go beyond style is ever more important. The fabric of old buildings is not only visually appealing but retains information about how people lived, how they worked and what they valued; it also has an amazing capacity to evoke memories. The relationship between an individual building and the city, town or village in which it stands is equally important. Giving new life to old buildings has the capacity to lend rootedness and continuity to a place while also reviving economic and community wellbeing.

VALUING CHANGE AND ADDITIONS

The introduction of new design elements tends to be thought of as an additive process. In reality it is also subtractive as, through necessity, some existing elements are invariably affected. Good designers do not happily sacrifice old fabric without reason. Those involved in conservation think hard about loss and change but this does not mean that all old fabric is inevitably sacred.

Figure 1.08
Historic context and location informs the sense of place at Chiddingfold, Surrey.

A conservation approach begins from a position that historic fabric of all dates and types may hold interest, but the strength of this interest can be weighed against the long-term benefits of change.

Widespread public awareness and interest in design has blossomed in recent years and it can be no coincidence that design perceptions have shifted with the explosive growth of image consumption. It is through images that buildings are often first experienced, be they on the web, in magazines or through television. These images are often inspirational, encouraging the notion of 'grand designs' and the idea that buildings can be radically changed and adapted. Potentially, this results in old buildings being damaged through lack of understanding but it also creates valuable awareness of the built environment, heritage and the potential of old buildings to have a continuing beneficial use.

What the experience of the image lacks is the visceral, haptic, physical nature of seeing and entering a real building. Becoming acquainted with a tangible structure is totally immersive, heightening the senses to the intensities of texture, light, shade, detail, colour, the patina of age and even sound and smell. Added to this may be the context of the building in terms of its sense of place, community and landscape. All of these things are essential contributory factors to the indefinable atmosphere of a building. Together they create impressions and help make memories that will be carried forward. The aesthetics of transformation must therefore respond to more than the photo opportunity. A well-executed design will connect with the ambience of the existing building, while not pretending to be part of the old or declaring itself self-consciously as a new object. It is not the false distinction resulting from the relationship between the new and the old that is interesting. It is, instead, the new whole that has been created: the atmosphere rather than the bold statement, the layering of past and present.

Defining change

Change in old buildings is defined in many ways. Good examples do not necessarily shout that they are different. Instead they engage and have a relationship – which may not immediately be obvious – with the existing structure, form and materials. This can be seen in a method of repair often associated with old buildings and the SPAB: tile repairs. These have long been employed as a means of consolidating decaying masonry due to their ability to be modelled to the eroded profile of the historic fabric and because they clearly show where change to the original structure has occurred.

The technique involves laying clay plain tiles in mortar and keying them to the sound core of the stonework. AR Powys, former SPAB secretary, describes the result in his book *Repair of Ancient Buildings*, first published in 1929: *'The material is very durable, the surface is plastic and can be modelled to fit adjoining stones, it is so keyed to the stone backing as to become a part of it, and the finished texture and colour are not objectionable, and "weather" pleasantly.'*

Figure 1.09
A traditional SPAB tile repair – functional and clearly showing where change to the original structure has occurred.

Similar repairs can be made with stone tiles. These have the same ability to stabilise crumbling masonry and offer readability but on a stone building do not visually jump out as being different. The principle behind tile repair is developed in projects such as Astley Castle, the Landmark Trust property in Warwickshire. Here, carefully selected brick consolidates the eroded edges of the structure and acts as walling within the reconstruction.

Tile repair is merely one technique used to express SPAB ideas and there are many other ways in which repairs may be made to work aesthetically while still delineating difference. In the renovation of the church of St Paul, Elsted, West Sussex in 1951, John Macgregor, a conservation architect and the then honorary technical adviser to the SPAB, successfully used different materials and introduced design features that had no historic precedent, including a distinctive hexagonal window, to define the new work to the building, while respecting what remained of the old.

Figure 1.10
Church of St Paul, Elsted, with newer materials and design clearly distinguishable.

The building had closed and become derelict after a new church was built in the mid-nineteenth century, although this too closed after a life of less than 100 years. In 1947 it became apparent that the unprotected Saxon walling of the nave was falling down. According to the SPAB's archives, a local resident, anxious to see such important remains preserved, sought the advice of the Society. The SPAB commissioned a full report, in which 'the great value of the Saxon masonry' was stressed and a strong plea made for re-roofing. As a result, Macgregor retained the surviving north wall of herringbone stonework, with two round-arched doorways filled in to make lancet windows. The new walls are of roughly squared ashlar outside and whitewashed brick inside, with a panelled roof. Macgregor incorporated an arch of 1622 in a new south porch, west of what appears from outside to be an aisle with a clerestory above, but is in fact a vestry. Instead of a belfry, a bell is hung from the east gable of the nave; in the west gable Macgregor inserted the new hexagonal window.

'The key to any alteration or redevelopment is understanding the building's historical evolution, from how it works now, its development through time, right back to its original core. Only then can you appreciate and capture its historical significance.'

Teresa Borsuk, Pollard Thomas Edwards

Of an altogether different scale, Bracken House in the City of London was built in the second half of the 1950s to house the headquarters of the Financial Times. The architect, Sir Albert Richardson, a SPAB member and conservationist, was in the Webb tradition, drawing heavily on historical influences and yet combining them in new ways. With Bracken House he brought new design – of a traditionally inspired kind – to bear in a highly sensitive historic context. Notably, when threatened with demolition in 1987, the building received a Grade II* listing, becoming the first post-Second World War structure to be protected in this way.

In the same year the building was sold and, with both the journalists and the printing works that it housed gone, Hopkins Architects was appointed to turn the building into modern office space. The printing works was replaced with a new block linking into the refurbished office wings and the entrance moved to the centre, its pink sandstone plinth and elliptical form allowing new build and old to merge to produce a coherent and functional new building in an important city location.

APPRECIATING HISTORIC INTEREST

Studying an old building's particular architectural qualities, its construction, use and social development is enlightening. Intimacy is essential, so investing time in close-up study beyond the desktop will almost certainly provide clues that will be useful when undertaking repairs or adding new elements. It will also help in understanding why decay sets in and how problems may be put right.

Before computer aided design (CAD), digital imaging and laser scanning, architects, surveyors and engineers came to have an affinity with, and be knowledgeable about, the structures with which they were involved because they were forced to measure and draw every detail on site. Today there is the danger that an electronic file of drawings and plans will arrive 'cold' on their desk and consequently they are removed from that opportunity to understand the idiosyncrasies, details and atmosphere of the building with which they will be working.

Figure 1.12
Grooves worn into the fabric of a church tower by decades of bell ringers' ropes – a detail that can be missed by electronic methods of assessing a building.

Clearly the accuracy and time savings provided by modern techniques are to be welcomed but it is important not to disregard the value of close-up, on-site understanding. A CAD survey will not, for example, pick up a season joint in brickwork where the original builders stopped work for the winter and, having capped the wall off to stop rain and frost penetration, had then not scraped mortar away before continuing the following season. This 'tidemark' may not have any practical value but it is an intrinsic part of the building's history and aesthetic.

LONG-TERM THINKING

Many buildings have remained unchanged for hundreds of years, partly because the demands placed on them have altered little and their fabric has been uncomplicated and simple to maintain. The speed of change is quicker today than ever before and it is easy to look at the immediate gain of adding new technology or embarking on adaptation and change without considering the validity of interventions in the longer term.

Work to buildings that will have only a relatively short-term benefit or will, by its nature, not be long-lasting is unlikely to be either sustainable or sympathetic to the fabric of the building. Inevitably, in the future, attempts will be made to reverse or modify changes and there will be a need to replace systems or components when they reach the end of their life. These ongoing interventions may, when judged against the future life of the building, happen over a relatively short period of time and, on each occasion, will invariably result in further loss of the structure's fabric and character.

Figure 1.13
Lifting this historic church floor for underfloor heating would cause irreparable harm.

One example of this process is underfloor heating, which is increasingly being considered in churches and houses. There are good reasons for its use: underfloor heating is seen as a sustainable and efficient solution that can reduce energy consumption, especially if used with renewable energy sources. Unfortunately, its installation in old buildings is likely to involve major upheaval and may have a significant impact on existing floor finishes and archaeology, while potentially changing the building's natural equilibrium when it comes to moisture control. In addition, these systems have a limited lifespan which may represent only a single generation. This might mean that the heating pipes have to be dug up and replaced, with all the inherent damage and loss that may result.

Similarly, the replacement or adaptation of centuries-old windows to accommodate double glazing aimed at improving thermal performance can be short-sighted when the average guarantee on the new unit is just ten years. Another controversial area is the substitution of leadwork with modern materials such as fibreglass which, while cheaper and less prone to theft, is a short-term solution and results in the loss of craft skills. Clearly, with any work, thought must be given to avoid potential opportunities being lost, while having consideration for the past and the future, as well as the present. A 200-year-old building may, after all, stand for another 200 years, and any work that compromises or does not take this possibility into account is almost certainly misguided.

PLACE AND COMMUNITY

Figure 1.14
Timber-frame upper ranges set over older stone walls in Winchester, Hampshire.

Individually and in groups, old buildings contribute richness and variety, helping to create places and communities. An awareness of the historic circumstance of their surroundings is essential: the traditional village green is as much about the buildings that surround it as the open space at its heart. Vernacular buildings in particular are products of local wisdom, climate and tradition. They are strongly related to the geography and history of a place, the lie of the land and the pattern of other development. Their styles reflect the materials found in the local landscape with the result that towns and villages may be categorised as being timber, brick or stone, thus contributing immensely to the sense of place and making them inseparable from the setting where they are found.

Retaining buildings in their setting enriches the character of an area and is essential to understanding the building's construction and the origins of its materials, craftsmanship and use. Conversely, integrity is undermined by dismantling and re-erecting these buildings in another location. Historic fabric is likely to be destroyed when a building is moved and the context is lost. All of this is important when considering new design and inevitably the approach will vary in every case. Should the response be to echo the existing material or should it consciously challenge the status quo, perhaps by introducing a new finish, material or colour?

Figure 1.15
East Beach Café, Littlehampton, a popular design and a contrast to the Victorian seafront.

In Littlehampton, West Sussex, Heatherwick Studio's East Beach Café, completed in 2007, may appear radical and a direct challenge to everything in its surroundings. In fact, it is a refreshing counterpoint to the Victorian seafront terraces and a welcome alternative to what could have been. According to the café's website: *'Before East Beach Café, there was a tiny kiosk on the site serving burgers, chips and nuggets. The owner got permission to turn it into a big restaurant, but the building he planned was not a pretty sight. Great for serving lots more chips and nuggets, but not of any architectural merit.'*

East Beach Café passed the planning process without a single objection, although such an approach may prove less acceptable in environments of close-knit historic buildings. Quite rightly, the criteria will subtly change to suit specific surroundings, but this is not to say that something fresh and responsive to the context would be out of place, provided it is well-mannered in form, function and proportion.

Regeneration

Regeneration of places in decline, through conservation combined with good new design, has been proven to work, reaping rewards for the economy of the local area and for the character and quality of the local environment. Even comparatively small projects bring benefits. East Beach Café gives a new reason to visit Littlehampton and brings new life to the resort. Local car park revenues are up 87 per cent, the town has new supermarkets and the café's owners are passionate about the power of business and design to change environments.

The creative re-use of old buildings can act as a catalyst to the process of regeneration, with successful schemes harnessing history, stitching together communities and drawing outsiders in. Urban Splash is a company that has been at the forefront of regeneration since the early 1990s with old, often listed, buildings at the heart of many of its schemes. Typically, these schemes are mixed use – involving residential accommodation, office space and leisure facilities – encouraging people to come in, see and use them. Often this involves making a new place, whether it is reinventing the historic Royal William Yard in Plymouth, Devon, the Rope Walks in Liverpool, the Lister Mills near Bradford or the 1930s Midland Hotel, Morecambe, which became a potent symbol of renaissance for the seaside town. In each case the focus has been as much on place-making as the individual buildings.

With the Grade I listed Royal William Yard the real challenge was not so much the buildings themselves – although there were inevitably challenges over cost and conservation – but the location. The development was on the 'wrong side' of Plymouth and, having historically been a victualling yard, there were perceptions about the surroundings, for example a red light district once existed nearby. For the scheme to succeed, the overall design quality had to be sufficiently high to bring in really good restaurateurs, businesses, residents and visitors to enjoy and use the buildings.

Good design has always been a vital ingredient for Urban Splash. Grade II* listed Park Hill, a former council housing block, is a landmark on the Sheffield skyline immediately to the east of the mainline railway station and city centre. When it opened in 1961 it was the most ambitious inner-city development of its time but by the 1980s the area was so run down and the perceptions so poor that it was on the brink of demolition.

'Buildings need to be allowed to breathe and express themselves. It's a very simple language about taking old buildings and analysing what's good about them. What's good about them you keep and you preserve and you respect, and what's not good about them you change. When you make that change it's unapologetically modern so it looks like it's been changed in the 21st century.'

Tom Bloxham, Urban Splash

Figure 1.16
Assertive design by Urban
Splash at Royal William
Yard, in Plymouth, working
with and around the
historic walls.

For the regeneration to succeed it was necessary, in this case, for Urban Splash to take a radical approach. This included losing much of the original interior to create a place for nearly 2,000 people to live, with offices, shops, a nursery, bars and restaurants below. The bold design strategy of architects Hawkins\Brown, working with Studio Egret West, transformed the modernist concrete landmark through the creation of new openings, the introduction of daylight and the use of colour.

In Bolton, Greater Manchester, the Churches Conservation Trust and OMI architects worked with local community leaders to transform the outstanding but unused Grade II* listed All Souls Church for the benefit of all who live and work locally. Standing at the heart of a multifaith community, the Victorian building reopened in December 2014 as a place for social enterprise. It welcomes all who venture through the door, including individuals who enjoy the café and activities, and local businesses who rent the facilities in the pods created inside the church for meetings and events.

Projects defined by good design, such as All Souls Bolton, have the potential to be hugely socially rewarding when undertaken in less affluent areas that suffer the additional challenge of aesthetic poverty in terms of modern design. Unless the motivation is strong, money to fund these projects and the political will to see them through is frequently diverted to focus on more direct needs, but by offering beacons of aspiration based on great new design the impact can be immense when a building is given a new future at the centre of a community. Embedding outreach, education and training from day one of such projects is essential. In the long term the building must be self-sustaining and capable of existing without subsidy.

Figure 1.17
Pods and a café within
All Souls Bolton.

Designing places

Good design in the historic environment involves maintaining interest, scale and a relationship with the buildings at its heart, while the spaces between and around the buildings provide their setting. The materials employed in these spaces often reflect the local vernacular and reveal patterns of wear and age while, below the surface, there may be a rich layer of archaeology.

Within the setting, the makeup of old paths, roads, hedges, walls and even signage creates context and interest, but appearance is not the only consideration: cobbles, for example, create a very different soundscape to gravel so a change in surface treatment can drastically affect the ambience of a place. Any new scheme must take these factors into account to ensure local character is strengthened rather than diminished and, just as with old buildings, a philosophy of repair, care and good new design is essential.

Although generally welcomed, traffic calming and pedestrianisation schemes need considerable thought as some alteration to the surfaces and spaces between buildings is inevitable. Appropriate selection of materials and layout is key. Block paving, for instance, can create sterile areas and a full carpet of identical wall-to-wall paving should also be avoided. Well-designed street furniture is important, as is the avoidance of unnecessary clutter caused by signage, bollards, planters and bins.

Figure 1.18
Streetscape in London's
Inner Temple, deriving
character from cobbles
and paving.

MATERIALS AND CRAFT SKILLS

Figure 1.19
Handmade bricks provide
a direct connection with
the maker.

The word 'craft' has the same meaning today as it did to William Morris. He sought simplicity and truth in a well-made thing: beautifully crafted buildings are at their best when they are uncomplicated and bear the mark of their maker. Craftsmanship sometimes seems expensive but it delivers pleasure in the long term. Match craftsmanship with high-quality, carefully selected materials and the building becomes distinct. Add to this good design and it is possible not only to embrace the here and now but to create a dialogue with the existing building and its context that reaches back through history.

A Georgian facade is not simply about proportion but also the beauty that springs from its subtlety and detail, brought alive by the craftsmanship of the bricklayer, joiner and mason. Imperfections are part of this; each glazing bar is uniquely formed, every pane of glass unintentionally distorted. We feel connected to the maker when we see a thumbprint in the clay of a brick or tile, the saw marks on a piece of timber, or the trowelling on an expanse of plaster.

CONSERVATION THROUGH DESIGN

Good design goes far beyond aesthetics. In many cases design innovation is vital to the conservation of old buildings due to the engineering solutions that it can offer, frequently in conjunction with new materials and technology. The use of these methods allows the integrity of the building to be maintained and as much historic fabric as possible to be retained while providing an honest approach that is easily readable in the future.

Figure 1.20
A thoughtfully designed
engineering intervention
to support 800-year-old
timber at Headstone
Manor, Harrow.

Headstone Manor in Harrow, west London, shows that the solution is often an architectural as well as engineering one. Here, the oldest part of the existing building is a very early timber frame of around 1310 in a surviving portion of the great hall. Its extreme fragility meant carpentry repairs would have created a huge loss of fabric and been quite destructive. The solution, devised by architect Francis Maude, a SPAB Scholar working at Donald Insall Associates, retains as much of the original fabric as possible.

Horizontal steel beams, which project beyond the building, were inserted beneath the wall plates and to these were attached steel uprights outside. This created a clearly expressed modern steel frame which holds the historic timber frame of the building in place. While initially quite startling, it is a good solution in conservation terms which has ensured that the building remains viable and succeeds in its new role as part of the Harrow Museum. The metalwork could have been entirely functional, but is thoughtfully designed where it projects from the building's exterior.

DIVERSE STYLES AND APPROACHES

The Firs, in Redhill Surrey, is what Nikolaus Pevsner, in *The Buildings of England* series, describes as '*a suave Regency-style house*.' What distinguishes it is the uncompromisingly modern wing, approximately the size of the older house, added by Basil Ward of Connell, Ward & Lucas in 1936. As Pevsner notes, this is a very early and very brave case of not '*keeping in keeping*'. He goes on to describe it as a '*perfect counterpoint between old and new, for example in the very careful but not servile relation of roof-lines, and the graded recession from the old to the new via the stair-well*'.

Very different, but nonetheless effective, was the approach taken by the architects Seely and Paget for Stephen and Virginia Courtauld at Eltham Palace in 1933–6. Here the new butterfly-plan house, with wings of red brick with Clipsham stone dressings, incorporated the medieval great hall, in the process adding layers of interest to what had been a ruin.

These were among the forerunners of the countless schemes that now exemplify the qualities of good new design within the historic environment. Some responses are bold and have fun with the new work, others are restrained and self-effacing; all can work equally well. The common theme is the need for a carefully considered relationship with the old building that is reflected in the composition, juxtaposition and huge investment in detailing of the elements that make the whole.

John Betjeman, Poet Laureate and SPAB committee member, humanised such thinking in a letter written to the architect of the National Theatre, Sir Denys Lasdun, in 1973 when the building was still unfinished: '*I gasped with delight at the cube of your theatre in the pale blue sky and a glimpse of St Paul's to the south of it. It is a lovely work and so good from so many angles.*'

The National Theatre is now an old and listed building in its own right and has itself been the subject of recent new work that demonstrates the power of good new design in the historic context. Be it the National Theatre or the renovation and reconfiguration of 25 Tanners Hill, Deptford, a timber-framed house by Dow Jones Architects; the 'eco-pods' inserted into the field barns of the Yorkshire Dales by Feilden Clegg Bradley Studios; Haworth Tompkins' vibrant Egg Theatre, created within the skin of a Grade II listed building in Bath; or the clever and subtle Refectory at Norwich Cathedral by Hopkins Architects, there is a common theme of creating innovative and interesting spaces that sit within and beside historic fabric without diminishing the context, values and narrative of the place.

Exceptional projects such as these are often described as exemplars but there is a danger in simply transplanting ideas from project to project. In reality, each scheme is different and requires a bespoke solution that respects and responds to the nature of the place and the individual building. There are no shortcuts to success; physically researching each building not only generates an essential understanding of its construction, materials and quirks, but also recognition that those now charged with its care will be similarly judged by generations to come.

Figure 1.21
Pevsner applauded the contrast between the new and the old at The Firs, Redhill.

Figure 1.22
The Norwich Cathedral
Refectory, completed in
2004.

CHAPTER 2:
STARTING POINTS

Any process to adapt or extend an old building should start by establishing the real need for change and ensuring this is set out in the brief. Fierce aesthetic and philosophical debate may be sparked and, for good new design to emerge, a creative and open relationship must be forged between all parties.

Buildings echo the evolutionary process that leads people and societies to adjust and diversify, with changing times reflected in buildings through modernisation, adaptation and everyday use. Simply touching a surface or walking on a floor results in alteration due to the action of wear which, although imperceptible day to day, grows to a patina of age over time.

Change in a building is often related directly to the aspirations and affluence of its owner and may be driven by fashion, necessity or new technologies. Tensions between the building and the occupants, such as lack of comfort or space, access issues, energy efficiency and aesthetics, are all factors. Outside influences are a further consideration. Shifting demographics, extremes of weather, economic cycles, legislation, wars and natural disasters all have an impact on buildings regardless of their history, type or function.

Buildings fall into a large number of categories, styles and ages. The careful thought that should be applied to the application of good design principles does not relate only to the UK's half a million listed buildings but to all buildings if they are to be aesthetically pleasing and practical.

Figure 2.00
The World Conservation and Exhibitions Centre extension to the British Museum, London, completed in 2014 (left).

Figure 2.01
A Georgian terrace in London's Bedford Square, now mainly converted to offices (right).

The process of achieving good new design in a historic context is subtle and painstaking, and certain basic principles provide a starting point. Helping the building find fresh life by working with, rather than against, the existing form is crucial, so the very first step is to acquire a deep understanding of the building: where it sits in the landscape, how it is constructed and how it performs. This relies on seeking clues in the history, fabric and structure of the building, evaluating what is there, and developing sensitivity to, and a better appreciation of, the context.

'Historic buildings need to be responsive to people's needs and they live by virtue of being used, as well as by simply being there. Therefore, the aspect of what it takes to use them to give them life is something which I'm disposed to feel is a reasonable starting point when approaching new design. The question then is, can you turn something which might be a problem into an advantage architecturally?'

Richard Griffiths, Richard Griffiths Architects

Figure 2.02
The reworked buildings that form Ditchling Museum, East Sussex.

DRIVERS OF CHANGE

Old buildings cannot always be preserved without change; extensions and adaptations are generally implemented as a means of allowing the building to function in a way that was previously difficult or impossible. This may be by adding more space, changing an existing space to make it more viable or creating a means of access or movement through or from the building. In all cases, the question must be asked: how can we best manage change?

The need for the new

The Victorian school buildings occupied since the 1980s by Ditchling Museum of Art + Craft in the village of Ditchling, East Sussex, had reached a stage where they were in very poor condition. The museum was consequently finding it increasingly hard to acquire new works, as it was impossible to guarantee the conditions in which the items would be kept. A point had been reached where a better-quality building was vital, as was the need to have a more public face. The idea proposed was to try to open directly onto the village green next to the site. The link with the place and setting was the starting point for the approach to the buildings and spaces of the museum. This underlies the fact that the museum is unusual in exhibiting a collection of art and craft objects connected to the artist and typographer Eric Gill and his group in the geographical place where they were made.

On London's South Bank, the National Theatre – a Grade II* listed building which opened only relatively recently in 1976 – is, at first sight, a fantastic work of architecture, so it may seem strange that adjustment is

Figure 2.03
The front entrance, to the National Theatre, London, originally intended to be accessible for people arriving by car.

necessary. Rewind through the past 40 years or so and the reason for that need becomes more obvious: not only has stage technology undergone profound change, so has the theatregoing experience.

Figure 2.04
The glass and metal facade of the National Theatre's new production workshop.

This is seen most obviously in the way audience members originally arrived. Sir Denys Lasdun, who designed the building, conceived the entrance with the motor car in mind and the presumption that the majority of audience members would drive, or be driven, to the front door, a concept that quickly became outdated. But the need for change went much deeper and the reasons are not hard to find. Theatre is a dynamic art form and for the NT to maintain its status as a world-leading theatre company, it needed to address new developments in the context of the building and in the facilities provided to audiences and backstage production teams. Public access, community involvement, education and outreach are all new kinds of social roles the NT and its buildings need to deliver.

Significantly, the National Theatre is two quite separate things: it is a vibrant, forward-looking theatrical production company that stages shows, but it is also a major work of static architecture which notionally could be frozen at a given moment in time. For Haworth Tompkins, the architectural practice responsible for transforming the building for NT Future – a six-year redevelopment programme completed in 2015 – there was the challenge of balancing the demands of these equally important entities. The response has opened up and made fresh sense of aspects of the building, enhanced its relationship with the surrounding environment, transformed the facilities for artists and visitors and allowed audiences much closer engagement with the theatre, both on stage and behind the scenes. Despite this, the firm imprimatur of Lasdun still resonates throughout the building.

Disaster

Not all buildings benefit from the luxury of planned change – for some, catastrophe is the driver. Fire, flood and war have inflicted heavy casualties on our built heritage, not least the bombing raids of the Second World War and the severe weather events of recent years. No building is immune: some are local tragedies, others are national disasters. Significantly, it is not just the fabric of the building that is damaged or lost but

often the associated contents and memories. Recovery can be hard and the obvious route to take is not always straightforward. After much of Chelsea Old Church in London was destroyed when a bomb fell nearby in 1941, the architectural historian, writer and SPAB committee member James Lees-Milne wrote, *'I do not believe we are justified in advocating the rebuilding of this particular church exactly as we believe it used to be. The spirit of the old church we knew can never be recaptured.'*

Figure 2.05
Chelsea Old Church, destroyed by bombing in 1941, as it is today.

Nevertheless, the church (whose chancel dated from the thirteenth century) was rebuilt in brick to the same scheme on the original foundations, with many of its tombs and fittings reassembled from fragments. It was reconsecrated in 1958. What is now found is a relatively modern construction, clearly of its time, but with strong echoes of what stood before.

A very different approach was taken in Coventry after the bombing of the city's fifteenth century Cathedral of St Michael in 1940. Here it was decided to build an entirely new cathedral alongside the ruins of the old and to turn the bombed nave into an unroofed garden of remembrance with the one surviving tower of St Michael's still used for bell ringing. The new cathedral, designed by Sir Basil Spence, was finished in 1962 and created an opportunity to include a substantial body of new art, sculpture, ironwork and stained glass by artists such as Graham Sutherland and John Piper.

The proposals and the design were the subject of great controversy at the time, even among well-informed SPAB members. A letter written in 1951 by Lord Esher to Monica Dance, who at the time were the SPAB chairman and secretary respectively, rebuffed a request for the Society to join the protest against the new plans for the cathedral. Lord Esher stated that he 'could not urge the Committee to do any such thing'. He went on to point out that the 'architect has no intention of touching any of the ruins' and that it would be contrary to SPAB principles to approve what the member would have liked to see: 'a complete reproduction of the old cathedral'. Once completed, the new cathedral was embraced as a symbol of renewal and reconciliation – and itself listed Grade I – with the old and new buildings effectively forming one body of architecture.

Redundancy

Throughout history, buildings have become redundant. Changing farming practices, the collapse of industries, shifting demographics and the coming of the internet have seen buildings as diverse as riverside warehouses, cotton mills, churches and high street banks lose their original purpose and face uncertain futures unless they can be adapted to a viable new use. When this fails, deterioration will surely follow as there is little economic reason to maintain the building and keep it windproof and watertight.

Traditional barns typify this trend, as very few meet the needs of the mechanised modern farm. In East Anglia alone, over 90 per cent of old barns have been lost either to demolition or conversion to other uses.

In the 1980s the SPAB's members undertook a significant survey of the remaining unconverted barns in the UK. Thanks to lobbying and awareness-raising by the Society, planning departments now try to encourage better solutions for empty barns, advice which is bolstered by good practice guides.

Many old hospitals, schools and prisons do not suit today's needs and in some cases face dilapidation and structural problems. In these cases, the economic and practical arguments sometimes become overwhelming and the facilities are moved to modern buildings which are easier to maintain and can accommodate state-of-the-art equipment, services and facilities.

The old buildings sometimes go on to form the core of successful new housing schemes with supplementary development alongside, as was the case at the King Edward VII Hospital near Midhurst, West Sussex. Built in 1901, the design for the buildings and the grounds was undertaken by an influential triumvirate of the day: Charles Holden, Henry Percy Adams and Gertrude Jekyll – a partnership linked to the Arts and Crafts movement. The hospital had been closed for some years when City & Country undertook a sympathetic renovation and conversion which resulted in the creation of 162 apartments, houses and communal facilities within the Grade II and Grade II* listed buildings.

In the case of All Souls Bolton, the Victorian church had been empty for around 25 years and had suffered vandalism and arson attack. The external repair bill was approaching £800,000, while the surrounding community had never seen inside. The original impetus for its conversion and re-use came from local people, who saw the building sitting empty and unkempt at the heart of their community. Interestingly, despite the Christian history of the building, the push to see the doors reopen largely came from the part of the community that was of Pakistani heritage, who saw beauty in the building and had a respect for its religious past. The campaign was successful and the church reopened in December 2014 as a place for social enterprise.

Figure 2.08
The former King Edward VII Hospital dining room is now a communal area for the surrounding residential apartments (far left).

Figure 2.09
The west entrance of All Souls Bolton. (left)

Ruin

Disaster and redundancy are among the calamities that lead to a building's long-term ruin. Many argue that ruins should be left as places of solitude, mystery and picturesque decay. This is particularly so when ruination marks a significant event, but it is not easy to maintain a particular fixed state of ruination. In the

Figure 2.10
A ruined church wall is stabilised with lime mortar before 'soft capping' with turf.

past – and even today – ruins have been plundered for their stone and other architectural salvage: the Colosseum in Rome was once leased as a quarry and marble from the city's ancient temples was burnt to produce lime.

Even if they survive such a fate, ruins pose many problems and managing decay is a key issue: should a ruinous structure be allowed to decay gradually or should it be preserved? John Ruskin, the Victorian art critic, thinker and early member of the SPAB, was a forward-thinking advocate of preserving ruins as ruins and leaving them as authentic historic relics. This option is far from straightforward, with vegetation and the weather – particularly frost damage – posing major problems. Even maintaining the appearance of doing nothing is difficult.

'Before we talk to the heritage bodies we try to think very carefully about what we want to do and have a very coherent argument of what we're trying to achieve, how we're trying to do it and why we need to make the changes. We find we have very positive conversations with them, particularly at high level. People understand that we have constraints about budget and cost and that we're typically working in areas of quite low value and we've got a desire to save the buildings and bring them back into use.'

Tom Bloxham, Urban Splash

Figure 2.11
St Luke's Church, London, in a ruinous state in the 1970s (right).

Figure 2.12
The shell of St Luke's Church was successfully adapted to a concert hall (far right).

The conversion and adaption of a ruin for use is equally challenging. Every ruin potentially inspires a variety of responses and part of the architect's job is helping it to fulfil a new need but in a form that speaks very much of the present. St Luke's, an eighteenth century church in Islington, London, designed by Nicholas Hawksmoor and John James, had been declared unsafe in 1959 following subsidence. The roof was subsequently removed, leaving the masonry shell a dramatic ruin. Levitt Bernstein became involved when the building was identified as a possible home for the London Symphony Orchestra's community and music education programme. The practice subsequently led a major and complex conversion to create a modern venue within the Grade I listed building, completed in 2003.

Astley Castle was in an even more decrepit state than St Luke's when the Landmark Trust, a building preservation charity, became involved in the 1990s. The sixteenth century fortified manor, which is Grade II* listed, had been gutted by fire in 1978. Vandalism, unauthorised stripping out and collapse had followed, leaving the building a ruin. The complexity and size of the site meant that previous proposals to save the building had failed so the charity's intervention was seen as a last chance.

When the Landmark Trust launched an architectural competition in 2007 *'to reinstate occupancy of Astley Castle in a manner appropriate for the 21st century'*, it did so recognising that its usual solution of conventional repair and conservation in order to create holiday accommodation was impractical, both technically and financially. The radical winning scheme by architects Witherford Watson Mann created modern accommodation within the ancient ruins in what the RIBA described as a prototype for a bold new attitude to re-use. Once realised, in 2012, the solution proved popular both with the public, who appreciated the design and the saving of the building, as well as the architectural profession, which recognised the technical and design challenges. The scheme won the Stirling Prize for architecture in 2013.

Social and demographic change

The fortunes of people and buildings are inextricably linked, and their destiny is frequently bound to politics and economics. History demonstrates that any building or individual can be affected. At one end of the social scale many stately homes were lost to the wrecking ball from the 1930s to the 1970s; at the other, whole swathes of inner-city housing were swept away during the massive slum clearance programmes of the 1960s.

Figure 2.13
Astley Castle, Warwickshire, was saved by the Landmark Trust and now provides holiday accommodation.

Some grand houses and estates have been saved through the determination of their owners, who have found ways to make them pay; others have been rescued by the National Trust or English Heritage or, in the case of houses like Compton Verney, by a charitable trust. There have been opportunities for new design in the form of visitor centres, extensions and internal alterations but these are nevertheless small in number when compared with the great mass of other old buildings undergoing change.

Worldwide, one million people move from rural to urban areas every week, so the pressures on city centres are intensifying. Existing buildings – both residential and commercial – have to be sensitively adapted and made to suit the needs and aspirations of those who inhabit them. Residential additions most clearly illustrate both the desire for the new and the pitfalls of poor design. In cities, in particular, the desire for extra space sees additions made outwards (rear or side extensions), upwards (loft conversions and penthouses) and downwards (basements) but this determination to gain space often places material considerations ahead of aesthetic ones.

There are other underlying and related trends, from the wish to have open-plan living areas, conservatories and media rooms to new double-glazed windows and external embellishments. This hunger for improvement is nothing new: the Georgians were keen to emulate classical styles so took delight in re-fronting timber-framed buildings in brick, sometimes faking the effect using mathematical tiles.

Despite the net movement of people from country to city, there is a smaller but significant migration to the countryside. Old buildings such as farmhouses or converted barns are seen as places for retirement or are invested in as holiday accommodation, while others find commercial uses or are tourist attractions. All are potential generators for creative re-use and some are excellent examples of good new design. Among the buildings that represent the biggest challenges are churches. Of the surviving buildings in the UK that are over 500 years old, the great majority are churches, with 45 per cent of all Grade I listed buildings in England places of worship. Their position is central and cherished in cities, towns and villages across the country.

WHY COMBINE OLD AND NEW?

Cultural, economic and societal changes mean that many buildings will not survive in their present state or in their present use so, in order to preserve these buildings for the generations to come, giving them new life is essential.

Figure 2.14
Vertical extensions, such as this one at the Clerkenwell Cooperage, London, are one way of providing additional residential accommodation in existing buildings (right).

Figure 2.15
All Souls Bolton, once again serving the needs of its local community (far right).

In recent decades designers, developers and institutions have realised that rather than being a burden, old buildings have the potential to be a valuable and sustainable asset. That said, the need for buildings to perform has never been as acute: real-estate values, energy efficiency and comfort rank high in any decision-making process.

Economic arguments

Poverty is sometimes said to be the best preserver of old buildings since change rarely occurs without available funds. While this is not altogether true, because maintenance is frequently neglected when times are hard, it is fair to say that economics plays a big part in driving change, especially in burgeoning cities, and money enables adaptation as families grow and businesses flourish.

With commercial buildings, the economics of making the building work comes into play to a far greater extent than with homes. Clients are naturally particularly keen to exploit floor areas to their full potential and this net-to-gross perspective can have a major impact on design considerations.

'Thinking about things that address the social, contextual and economic issues in and around a project is often as important as the way that you deal with the design. That kind of social and economic context is as significant as how you respond to the materials of the historic building or site.'

Liz Smith, Purcell

With two of Pollard Thomas Edwards' projects – the Granary for Rooff, in east London, and Gunpowder Mill for Hill, in Waltham Abbey, Essex – there was another consideration when considering the economics of the design strategy. Both clients are construction companies, so the buildings would provide showcases for their work.

Maintaining the volume of the internal space was particularly important at the eighteenth century Gunpowder Mill. Here, despite the loss of valuable floor space that might have been gained through division, Hill embraced Pollard Thomas Edwards' idea of retaining original machinery and maintaining the internal volume of the building through the insertion of bridges and platforms.

Conversions to residential use can pose unexpected problems. Buyers want charm and features but at the same time they expect spaces that suit their lifestyle, a difficult balance for property developers. Apartments are particularly tricky, as standard layouts rarely work, so the skill of the designer is to make each one bespoke by exploiting the quirkiness of the plan and ensuring each includes features that are special and related to the history or integrity of the building.

Undoubtedly, compared with building from scratch, converting an old building is more complicated and involves extra time and energy, but good design is not in itself any more expensive than bad, and the results bring rewards. The inherent qualities and the finite supply of old character buildings adds to their appeal and means they have the potential to rent or sell for a premium compared to new builds.

According to Historic England (*Heritage and the Economy*, 2016): '*Creative and cultural industries are 13 per cent more likely to be found in a listed than a non-listed building. Analysis of the leading commercial property data source, the Investment Property Databank (IPD), shows that investing in heritage has positive returns. Between 1980 and 2011, listed retail, office and industrial properties have generated total returns equal to or higher than their non-listed counterparts for 3, 5, 10 and 30 year periods.*'

Sustainability

Many old buildings have served well over decades, if not centuries, and have proved their adaptability and durability. Discussions about sustainability are generally concerned with quantifiable and objective aspects but there is a broader sense of the term that includes conservation value in retaining heritage, the continuity of spirit of a place and connections to human history and community; all are attributes that should not be given up lightly.

There are strong sustainability arguments in favour of retaining as much of the 'old' as possible and integrating new design rather than demolishing and starting afresh, not least to prevent the loss of embodied carbon locked within the materials and during the initial act of construction. Old buildings are intrinsically sustainable due to the natural materials and methods used to build them. These materials tend to be more recyclable and come with a lower energy cost than many modern materials and, in the case of timber, act as a carbon store. Traditional vernacular buildings are typically made with readily available local materials, safeguarding supply and skills and reducing transport costs.

Any proposed changes should be mindful of these facts. An early step is to consider how the special qualities of the building relate to its potential environmental characteristics; any development gains should be designed to enhance rather than detract from these.

Figure 2.16
Walkways and work areas
at Gunpowder Mill, Essex.

The aim of new build or retrofit associated with an old building is to increase its amenity and make it enjoyable and comfortable to occupy. The work carried out should enhance the overall value of the property in terms of utility, as well as aesthetically, financially and environmentally. To achieve this, the needs and attributes of the building must be balanced with the desire for performance and comfort. New work requires a considered approach and a light touch. Regular maintenance and gentle repair is vital to an old building, while all work must respect its history, character, the ability for it to be repaired and the part it plays in the wider community.

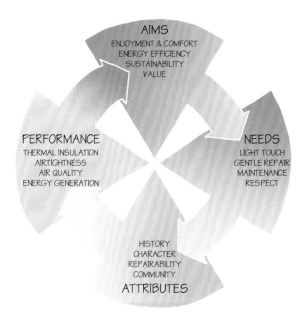

Figure 2.17
The virtuous circle of sustainability relating to old buildings.

Energy efficiency is a valid priority. Retrofitting a building to increase its performance might include improving its thermal insulation and airtightness, ensuring good indoor air quality and providing a means of energy generation. There are increasingly well-documented solutions to such issues, although they need careful research and sensitive implementation. When combined, all of these factors create a virtuous circle. Each one is reliant on the other; when considered and implemented together, the overall effect is to increase the sustainability of the whole building.

From the outset, the decision-making matrix must consider which options are available to make the building more sustainable and then which of these can and should be employed and exploited to achieve maximum potential for the scheme. Various checklists and certifications – including BREEAM and LEED – play a useful role in benchmarking how old and new buildings can be improved, although it should be noted that these were not initially devised for assessing buildings built in traditional ways, so their use must be treated with a degree of caution. Typically, three main points should be considered:

» The building envelope. Can this be made more thermally efficient without an impact on external and internal aesthetics?

» The mechanical and electrical installations within the building. Can these be made more efficient through maintenance, upgraded equipment and better control?

» Energy generation and resources. Can elements of the building be taken 'off grid' through energy generation, water treatment and the use of surrounding resources?

Additions to old buildings should, unless there is a deliberate plan for them to be ephemeral, be built for the long term, thus engendering sustainability and minimising future disturbance to the existing building and its site. With this in mind, the new work should be designed and built to the highest possible specification, with consideration given to the possibility of using natural materials, particularly those that work well with traditional construction.

Careful choice of material potentially results in impressive carbon savings, as is illustrated at the Garden Museum, which occupies the medieval and Victorian church of St Mary-at-Lambeth, in London. Here the use of a cross-laminated timber (CLT) structure took the equivalent of some 200 tonnes of CO_2 out of the atmosphere.

'Redesigning old buildings is a sustainable thing to do providing you make them perform environmentally better than they were doing before. It's about finding the right thing for that building, for that client and for that project on a case-by-case basis.'

Adam Richards, Adam Richards Architects

Figure 2.18
Cross-laminated timber has been extensively used at the Garden Museum in the church of St Mary-at-Lambeth, London.

PHILOSOPHY AND ETHICS

Inevitably, the philosophy and ethics of placing new design in the historic environment are sometimes questioned. Fundamentally, a question can be asked as to whether the historic built environment should be subject to change at all. But, apart from those few buildings that are of such merit that static conservation is the appropriate response, all other buildings must face either eventual decline or, at some point, the prospect of change and adaptation in order to extend their life.

Philosophical and ethical arguments for preserving historic fabric have been made since the mid-nineteenth century, formalised in the SPAB Manifesto of 1877, and expanded in the twentieth century ICOMOS charters formulated at Athens, Venice and Burra. Between them, they have established the importance of authenticity and the idea of the built heritage as a cultural legacy to be carefully handed on. While the initial driver for these was in response to the highest-profile buildings and archaeological sites, such as the Acropolis, the principles can be applied to any building. The 1979 Burra Charter in particular includes useful definitions as to what exactly is meant by such terms as preservation, restoration and reconstruction, as well as introducing the idea of cultural significance. Another reference is BS 7913:2013 *Guide to the Conservation of Historic Buildings,* which describes best practice in the management and treatment of historic buildings. It applies to historic buildings with and without statutory protection and lays out all stages, from initially looking at a building through to the completion of appropriate work.

In practice, when faced with the problems of a particular building, the thinking found within the SPAB Manifesto and these other documents is of immense help when deciding on a course of action, whether planning an overall scheme or handling details of work. For example, the question might arise as to whether original fabric can be sacrificed where a new brick course meets original stonework to enable whole rather than cut bricks to be accommodated, thus creating a look that is neat and considered. In this case, agreed conservation principles would advise that new should always be adapted to fit the old, so the original fabric should be retained and the new brickwork planned accordingly.

'Older buildings have surface quality and uniqueness and make their mark as fragile, scarce, rare, authentic, beautiful things. Modern buildings are, in most cases, significant because of the design intent, the technological achievement or the political moment in which they were created. An old building we would gently repair. Although every case is different, with a modern building we would instinctively seek to restore it, to make it look as if it were brand new because we empathise with the aspiration of the designers and the team to create something that was of its time.'

Geoff Rich, Feilden Clegg Bradley Studios

Figure 2.19
A balance between new
and old at Astley Castle,
Warwickshire.

Good decisions come only with clear understanding, both of the building and the thoughts and principles that have been devised and refined over the decades. It is not as simple as imagining a polarisation between the 'new and clean' and the 'old and dirty'. As today's new buildings become tomorrow's old stock, these questions will continue to be asked. The design of modern buildings leads to issues of what they are going to look like and how they are going to be cared for in the future.

ARCHITECTURAL OPPORTUNITIES

Attempts to balance the needs of legislation, conservation, sustainability and the requirements of what some call the 'heritage police' tend to stifle imagination. The best schemes arise when the qualities of the old building are harnessed and celebrated through a creative dialogue between the planning authorities, the client, the designer and the other key professionals and bodies.

At the outset there are many questions to ask: How old is the building? How complete is it? What is it made from? What is the proximity of it to other structures or landscapes? What part does it play in the wider community? What is the purpose of the building and the planned addition or intervention? Expanding on these themes and having the opportunity to create new chapters in the story of a building contributes to the joy of designing in the historic environment. Some of the best projects use history as their motivation.

In Gloucestershire, a redundant listed gasworks was bought with planning permission to occupy only the upper parts of the roof space of the original building. In reality, this scheme was impractical and could not

Figure 2.20
The Gasworks,
Gloucestershire, a
combination of creativity
and conservation.

be realised without compromising the building's character. The idea to extend was first suggested by the conservation officer.

Chris Dyson Architects took inspiration for the Gasworks directly from the site. The new buildings extend out in an L-shape to create a courtyard, open to a field on one side and with a cylindrical tower at one corner that houses two writing rooms. This references the old carbide gas cylinder that originally stood on the site, its position now marked by a circle that forms a curve in the plan.

With Astley Castle it was realised early on that the destruction that had happened in the past was actually an asset rather than a liability. The new building has grown from the historic core of the oldest part of the ruin and has added continuity and context while focusing on maintaining the sense of life within the castle and making the most of the views both into and out of the site. Similarly, Donald Insall Associates enabled an effective re-use within the ruined towers at the Grade I listed Blencowe Hall, near Penrith, Cumbria. The large gash in the south tower is reputed to have been the result of attack in the English Civil War and, as such, is evidence

'There has been some good-quality thinking among the conservation bodies in recent years which trickles down. Whereas a planner is just thinking in terms of ticking boxes regarding various requirements, from size of footprint to materials, you can often have your best discussions with conservation officers because they're thinking in a broader sense of history.'

Chris Dyson, Chris Dyson Architects

Figure 2.21
Blencowe Hall, Cumbria, now provides holiday accommodation.

of a significant historic event that deserves to be retained. In design terms, it was seen as an opportunity to create a striking intervention that enhanced the existing fabric and brought the tower back to life. The structure was consolidated and new roofs, a staircase and new floors were added within the ruin while the gash in the wall was stabilised by the insertion of recessed balconies. Unlike Astley Castle, the intervention is set back behind the historic walls rather than built into them.

Among the successes of All Souls Bolton are the internal vistas and viewing angles that were never available historically: a large picture window in one of the pods that looks down over the choir stalls and a view from a staircase to the west end both allow new chances to discover and experience the building.

CLIENTS

In the minds of some clients, an old building, while highly desirable, can also equal known and unknown costs, limitations and risk. The truth behind the adage that *'you should live with an old building rather than make it live with you'* may simply be impractical as a new owner tries to make it a place that is immediately useable.

An architect who is familiar with the historic environment is well positioned to work with a client to build the confidence necessary to create a design that respects the original structure. 'Negotiating' between the client and the building is a key part of the architect's job and the process allows the client to embrace the conceptual and intellectual framework that guides the approach to a successful project. Clients need to feel proud of the building they occupy and to be confident of themselves and their role within it. Essentially, it is about the building being an intrinsic part of what they are and how they see themselves.

The positive impact that a self-aware and well-informed client can have on a project cannot be overemphasised. Working with an articulate and

'With the Garden Museum, one of the main things we were trying to achieve through the design was to allow the museum as an organisation to find an identity which enabled them to get their heads above the parapet, literally and metaphorically. What's been interesting is the way that the architecture enabled them to break the shackles of the building and this has enabled them to be a lot more reflective about the building that they have.'

Alun Jones, Dow Jones Architects

Figure 2.22
New material woven into the structure, providing meeting and exhibition spaces for the Garden Museum.

sensitive client – and one who has thought about the brief before involving an architect – will result in conversations that are thoughtful and productive, particularly if they love and value the building, and it is possible to draw on their knowledge of how it works and feels. Quick decisions often need to be made as work to historic fabric progresses and unexpected problems occur, so it is also beneficial if the client has an understanding of conservation philosophy. Where the client is a large organisation, it is important to establish who the key decision-makers are early on and to build trust and a dialogue with them. With the cooperation of the client and their clear grasp of the project, the design focus can be maintained in the search for solutions when there is a time pressure.

'It's very much a team effort, it's not all from me. I drive the philosophy of the practice but the efforts of individuals involved – of project architects and of craftsmen like bricklayers – have to be acknowledged; they're essential in the making of a well-made building and allow us to achieve a high level of quality. Procurement is very important to this process.'

Chris Dyson, Chris Dyson Architects

THE PROCESS OF PROCUREMENT

The need to balance factors of quality, cost and time must always be remembered when procuring work. Fortunately, when dealing with historic buildings, quality in the original is generally a given but with quality, and the sometimes unpredictable nature of work to old buildings, comes inevitable cost and time implications. Collaboration between owners, occupiers, designers and contractors is essential. On many projects there is an intense commitment to pursue quality, and those involved often go beyond the call of duty and have a determination not to sacrifice integrity in the pursuit of the right solution.

Ideally, as much detail as possible will be designed up front. There will be a deep understanding of the building and a good estimate of the costs will have been made before tendering begins. Many contractors will provide significant input and some form of design-and-build or management contract route may be adopted. When working with trusted contractors, a day rate may be appropriate, especially where costing is difficult due to the unpredictability of working with old buildings, particularly at the early stages of a project. In such cases a mechanism for controlling costs without describing the scope of the work may be employed. Working with old buildings can involve a considerable amount of site work for architects and other professionals because of the 'unknowns' that may emerge during a project, and this should be factored in when calculating fees. At the same

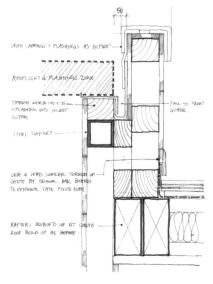

Figure 2.23
Junctions and weatherproofing considerations for the Copper Kingdom Centre, north Wales showing the typical level of detail required.

time it is essential that good craftspeople are given the space to put their skills into practice. Many are highly experienced in working with historic structures and are expert problem solvers in their own right, knowing the techniques that will deliver the desired outcome.

WHO IS QUALIFIED TO DO THE WORK?

From designer to contractor, every client needs to find the most suitable person or team to do the job. This need is not exclusive to projects involving old buildings but the consequences of making the right decisions can be hugely beneficial and are perhaps more pronounced where a historic structure is involved. For modern architecture successfully to be introduced into the historic context, there is a need for people with skills and experience that embrace both an understanding and sometimes highly specialist knowledge of building conservation and the advantages of good new design.

The help of a historical researcher can be a useful first step in making sense of the building at a pre-design stage. A good architect will appreciate the building's history and take it forward in a new and creative way. This requires an appreciation of craftsmanship, period detailing and the ability to analyse and repair the old. Working with old buildings frequently demands a practical and somewhat pragmatic approach, and projects are rarely the same. Whatever the age of the building there are likely to be surprises. Even in a precisely proportioned Georgian terrace, houses will not be identical in construction and later adaptations or additions will present further challenges needing understanding and detective work.

The appointment of the right professionals is key and when creating new work in a historic context it is not unusual to have a conservation architect and a designer versed in contemporary idioms working alongside one another. Indeed, if the range of skills cannot be found in one person, a collaboration between conservation architects and design studios is increasingly seen as the best way to create exciting architecture.

Professionals with conservation accreditation or training from appropriate bodies should always be preferred. Peer-review of professional skills is increasingly undertaken and there are now more than 1,200 formally accredited conservation practitioners in the UK. The professional body conservation accreditation schemes include those run by the RIBA, AABC and RIAS for architects, RICS for surveyors, CIAT for architectural technologists and CARE for engineers. The SPAB runs the Lethaby Scholarship training programme in practical building conservation for young architects, surveyors and engineers, while its William Morris Craft Fellowship provides training for craftspeople employed in the repair of historic buildings on site or in workshops.

Conservation architects

There is a gradation to the level of intervention in any conservation approach which will vary with the building involved. At one end of the spectrum the work will be geared to the pure and very precise task of preserving the building and its fabric; at the other end a radical degree of change and replacement may be necessary. While some see the work of conservation and modern architects as clearly separate, there is a danger in polarisation, as this can compromise technical, aesthetic and philosophical priorities.

Figure 2.24
A Georgian terrace in Bath: even houses that look identical each have their own idiosyncrasies.

The role of the conservation architect is one that has developed. In the post-war period, the architectural theorising of the day was still promoting the idealism of the modern movement, believing the old world should be torn down and a better, new world built. This suggested a notion that architects do not look after old buildings but, instead, build new ones in a style that is radically unlike the old. In reaction to this a body of conservation architects emerged that sought to preserve and protect old buildings, but some had little sympathy with or understanding of new buildings. Today the divisions are less firmly drawn and many architectural practices specialise in both conservation and new design; although often designers without this dual knowledge – not all of whom are architects – are appointed to adapt buildings and the conservation element is added as an afterthought.

A good conservation architect will maintain intellectual control of a project and be capable of undertaking emergency repairs to a collapsing building and then be able to move on to drawing and designing the building, producing the working drawings and executing the works with a building contractor and, where appropriate, another designer.

'What conservation architects bring is humanity, understanding, expertise and, most of all, an awareness of what is technically possible on building sites by skilled craftspeople who often know more about their materials than the people specifying them. I learned this on a SPAB Scholarship where, in the morning, you may get shown something by an architect or a surveyor and, in the afternoon, you appreciate what the craftsperson actually does with that specification. In some cases they're not doing what they're told, instead it's ten times better!'

Geoff Rich, Feilden Clegg Bradley Studios

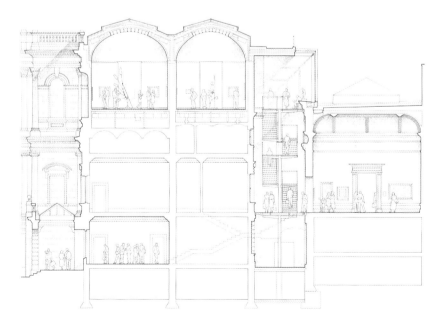

Figure 2.25
Royal Academy of Arts'
Sackler Galleries, London,
a collaboration of
conservation and new
design.

True and lasting collaboration between conservation and design architects can be rewarding and significantly strengthen the overall team. An example of successful collaboration is the Royal Academy of Arts' Sackler Galleries in London. Here conservation practice Julian Harrap Architects worked with Foster + Partners towards a solution which is based on the fact that the original Palladian building falls within an intellectual framework of classicism. While there is substantial new design within the scheme, the aim was to intervene with history in order to help the spectator grasp the meaning of the building without consciously highlighting the new and the old.

Together with the research-based element of their role, conservation architects have a thorough grasp of the sector's current thinking and have ready access to research on repair techniques and appropriate materials. They should have a good relationship with the heritage bodies involved, which is especially useful when producing the conservation and other statements necessary with many projects in order to obtain planning permission and listed building consent.

In some cases a conservation architect can help achieve a more radical solution than would otherwise have been possible because they can argue its validity. To achieve these goals, other professionals may also be called upon, such as specialists who will analyse original paint microscopically to understand the colour and composition of the layers and chemically to reveal the pigments used.

Surveyors

Surveyors well versed in old buildings play a significant role in ensuring a successful marriage between historic fabric and new work and can enhance opportunities for good new design. Their ability to provide fault diagnosis and suggest remedies and repairs is often vital and they may act as a sounding board within the context of a team when considering the appropriateness of interventions. Surveyors can preempt questions and objections that may be raised and possibly alter and amend original designs to still give the same end result but using a different approach. This way of working can allow the designer to come forward with a proposal and for the surveyor to suggest modifications that enable more historic fabric to be retained while still enabling the design intent to be achieved.

Structural engineers

Concerned with all elements of a building's physical integrity, the role of structural engineers in projects involving old buildings is highly valuable and their special expertise often enables design innovation that would otherwise be impossible. In the case of Astley Castle, Price & Myers was responsible for providing engineering solutions that included stabilising the existing rubble walls with anchors, rebuilding retained edges with brick diaphragm walls in lime mortar, the use of precast concrete, carefully detailing exposed roof timbers, and the installation of a hanging timber staircase.

Builders and craftspeople

Many builders are no longer builders in the strict sense of the word; they are management contractors who employ specialist subcontractors. This approach can work, but employing a builder who understands the vocabulary of materials, who knows the full scope of trades and has a regular team is more likely to produce good results. Skilled craftspeople have a huge depth of knowledge and will range from masons and joiners to woodcarvers and lead workers. These people also often have a good appreciation of new design and the opportunities it brings by maintaining interest in their specialism and sustaining skills and training.

'The language of craftsmanship is the same whether you're building clunch walls or boat building. The ability to work with timber, GRP, stainless steel, aluminium and so on is really just a translation of materials. The skill base is similar.'

Julian Harrap, Julian Harrap Architects

Figure 2.26
Craftspeople with traditional or modern skills are essential to the success of a building project.

Generally, any separation between professionals and the craft practitioners is imagined; there is mutual reliance and mutual respect. Many old buildings were constructed without an architect's input as we now understand it. It was craftspeople, as master builders, who designed and built many great cathedrals, while most vernacular buildings result from local craft traditions and knowledge passed down through generations.

Figure 2.27
A detailed conservation plan was produced before work began on refurbishing and extending BBC Broadcasting House, London.

NEW DESIGN FOR OLD BUILDINGS

CONSERVATION PLANS

A conservation plan provides a means of identifying the most significant features and places where care needs to be taken, as well as those areas that are less significant. The plan may convey a hierarchy of importance graphically through, for example, a coloured key of red, amber and green. The plan should be a standalone document which can be built upon as more knowledge becomes available. Some are the work of one person, who might be an architect, others are a team effort embracing a number of disciplines.

As well as considering the building and its site, the plan will, where appropriate, help clarify the building's value, not only architecturally but at cultural, political, economic and artistic levels, so it takes a skilled hand to pull these strands together to produce a meaningful document. As time goes on, the conservation plan may grow as more knowledge becomes available, perhaps about the design, the builder and the people who have used the building. A plan should be impartial and undertaken to inform the design or the interventions but not written to enable a predetermined design or particular set of works. Understanding gained from a conservation plan is translated into policies that will guard and retain the values that make the building significant in the long term.

MEASURING SUCCESS

Judgements on whether a project is successful are often based on first impressions. In reality, the true outcome of a scheme may not be known for some years as good design is not just focused on the present but is about whether the building is enjoyed and used, how it is maintained and whether it has proved viable and durable. One of the reasons different periods of intervention in earlier buildings are often appreciated is simply that they have worked and are familiar and loved.

'A conservation plan can help determine a building's historic significance and allows you to assess the impact of alterations on the building. It doesn't say you must not take the roof off Broadcasting House or you must not build in the most valuable bit of a castle, but rather that we recognise that these are the most significant parts of the building. With Broadcasting House we carried out extensive historical research and produced a plan that stated our definition of what's important. Obviously first was the building itself; secondly there were the interiors and the question of whether they were of architectural merit; thirdly it was the question of whether they were of cultural of artistic interest. Then we graded them in importance.'

Mark Hines, Mark Hines Architects

CHAPTER 3:
CONSIDERATIONS FOR SUCCESS

Understanding the historic fabric and structure, and considering the implications of interventions or new additions, will produce the most successful methodology for adaptation. Most important of all is the relationship between old and new in terms of style and mass, and the consideration of detail, such as how junctions are designed.

There are many routes to making new work in a historic context successful. As with all good architecture, there is a requirement for high-quality, sensitive design, visual clarity, carefully selected materials, the intelligent development of ideas and an understanding of place and context. The question must always be asked: *'What is the intent, the quality of the space and the atmosphere desired?'* The response will be subjective and creative but should still in some way resonate with the historic fabric.

Designing for the historic environment inevitably introduces complications and requires all aspects of the existing building or buildings to be thoroughly understood and sympathetically analysed. This is about more than just data gathering. It is an organic, sensory process that involves intimacy with the existing structure where seeing, touching and engaging with the fabric, while mentally peeling back the layers, brings the reward of deep understanding.

Essential to the design strategy is a responsive and layered approach constructed on the foundation of this knowledge. The designer must juggle respect for the old building with the needs of the new in order to fulfil the requirements of the brief, while answering the necessity with any project that it must be practical, sustainable and built on time and within budget.

A clear grasp of the nature of old buildings and conservation philosophy will help guide design strategies and the way they are implemented on site during the course of a project, helping to maintain what is special while informing the new.

'Good new design is a continuity of good past design. I don't see these things in compartments. We have always built with the materials and the techniques we have, with the services and with the memories we have; they change as history moves on, as do people's perceptions and ideas.'

Sir Donald Insall, Donald Insall Associates

With some old buildings the approach will, of necessity, be sober, allowing for little visible change; with others it will find the freedom to do something that is defining, modern and distinctive. New work will add fresh layers and, if done well, will augment the building's history and importance, reflecting social, cultural and economic change through time.

Figure 3.00
Martello Tower Y on the Suffolk coast.

UNDERSTANDING, RESPECT AND SYMPATHY

One of the most important roles for anyone charged with caring for and working with an old building is to become its guardian. The surviving fabric of any existing building is finite and, once destroyed, can never be retrieved. Consequently, it is essential to consider carefully the direct and indirect consequences of every action when undertaking work because the value attached to the building may be seriously harmed. Minimising the loss of historic fabric and ensuring, as far as is possible, that what is introduced is at least as good and as equally appreciated as that which is lost should always be the aim.

Gathering information and recording through surveying, photography and report writing are vital first steps in order to understand as much as possible about a building, for example: its history, significance, development, condition, construction and performance. Old buildings can reveal as much information as historical documents: later additions, erosion of surfaces and the patina of age say much about how the building has been used and what has happened to it.

Initial appearances are often deceptive. Externally, Martello Tower Y, on the Suffolk Coast, converted into a family home by Piercy&Company in 2010, seems to be a simple structure. In reality its walls, dating from 1808, are 3m thick brickwork containing a rabbit warren of ducts and voids that provided ingenious 'air conditioning' from the roof to the soldiers who would have once occupied the lower floor.

As well as from the building itself, sources of information include: maps; records from the construction of the building, including legal documents; later surveys and reports; and diaries and the memories of those who have occupied and worked on and in the building.

New owners are advised to live with an old building through all four seasons before doing anything. This allows for a period of learning: how the light hits the walls and penetrates the interior, where the cracks are and whether they change over the course of the year, how the layout of rooms and spaces works, what is

Figure 3.01
The Pod Gallery is a modern exhibition space in a former barn, created with little visible change to the exterior of the building (far left).

Figure 3.02
An old gatehouse in Norfolk, with the years of major works visibly recorded (left).

really valuable and what is not. When introducing new design elements, all these factors count and need to be considered, if not experientially, then at least through careful analysis of the facts.

Crucially, the design processes may be very different to those associated with new construction. With new buildings, the majority of the detailing can be committed to paper well in advance of construction and the necessary planning and building regulation approvals will be set at an early stage.

A difficulty with old buildings is that an analysis of the structure prior to intervention can often only garner a limited amount of information. Much may be hidden, site safety might preclude thorough examination and intrusive or destructive investigations can be required that are only possible as work proceeds.

Revisions may be required to designs and regulatory approvals as evidence of the building's structure or history is revealed. This is not always easy when faced with the naturally protective and perfectly understandable desire of a regulatory authority to have before them a definitive scheme, and is naturally unnerving for those financing the works.

'First, we like to befriend the building, finding out how it came to be, what it is, and the trends within it. The other considerations are the ownership, occupancy and use of the building; not only now but looking forward, and how in fact it is meeting the goals and requirements that the owner has in mind. It's like a marriage-broking exercise between the changing continuity requirements of the structure and those of the owner or user; very possibly also bearing in mind that one day there will be other owners and users – that's the tricky bit.'

Sir Donald Insall, Donald Insall Associates

Listed buildings obviously pose the greatest challenges, none more so that the Grade II* listed Astley Castle in Warwickshire. To bring clarity to a scheme that involved not only consolidating the ruins left after a disastrous fire but also inserting modern accommodation within the walls necessitated balancing listed building consent with good sense. This required trust and flexibility between the conservation bodies, architect and client. Deferring decisions where necessary created space for reflection and decision-making at the appropriate time.

Figure 3.03
The timber frame of a much earlier structure was discovered after work started on this Victorian house.

At the National Theatre, one of the foundations for the project's success was that the team from Haworth Tompkins did not make decisions until they had been involved with the building for some time. They were commissioned to produce a conservation management plan and this helped establish their relationship with the building, not least by meeting the other people who cared about it and making sure everyone was in accord.

This period of calm was fundamental in providing the chance to understand the building before making the decisions that would change it. Consequently, it was possible to gain a deep understanding of the existing architecture, see how it worked and appreciate the goals of the project before a brief was produced. This meant that the design team saw what they were tasked with from an unusual angle. Importantly, rather than viewing it from the outside as a site and an opportunity to make their mark, they were starting from within the building with a body of sympathetic knowledge.

The result was a layered series of approaches relating specifically to parts of the building under consideration and what interventions were needed. All of the decisions that followed were made with respect to Denys Lasdun's own, very clear hierarchical thinking about what the building was made of and how it was composed.

When additions are made to a building, the process may require consideration of the setting and active engagement between disparate but important elements, as is the case with BBC Broadcasting House in central London. Here the original Grade II* listed 1932 Art Deco building links with the new structure, which sweeps around in a cyclorama-like form, creating a theatrical backdrop behind the nineteenth century, John Nash-designed, All Souls Church.

This modern facade, with its strong urban context, binds the historic buildings with the new. It also doubles as an external studio backdrop during events such as election night broadcasts. Such design also demonstrates how an iconic old building and its additions can become integral to the identity of an organisation or brand.

Working on such schemes is exhilarating as well as daunting and quite unlike creating a new building on a greenfield site. The emphasis on detail is exceptional, with the process ultimately involving a huge series of tiny decisions that might be to do with colour, tone, texture, finish and a host of other considerations but all with constant reference to the context and fabric of the older structure.

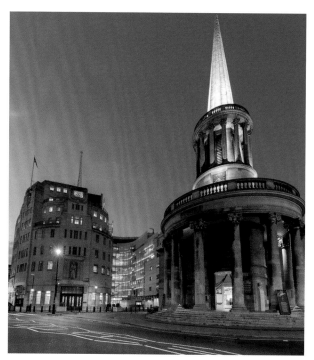

Figure 3.05
The new form of BBC Broadcasting House, London, responds to the neighbouring All Souls Church in Langham Place.

CONSERVATION PHILOSOPHY

'Thinking before acting' is the key tenet of conservation philosophy. Age can confer beauty of its own, so respect and care are the watchwords, with the emphasis on keeping as much of the original fabric as possible. Good repair takes account of bulging, bowing, sagging or leaning elements and, although seeking to ensure structural integrity, does not attempt to iron out, smarten or hide imperfections. A good repair should result in minimum further loss of fabric.

There is a danger of sanitising old buildings through cleaning and overzealous management. Every action must be justified and defensible and kept to a minimum. A balance should always be struck between competing approaches, principles and ethics; authenticity and integrity are key.

There are some basic guiding principles:

» Respect the beauty and imperfections of age.

» Retain original fabric and surface patina.

» Respect historic alterations and additions.

» Conserve rather than restore, repair rather than replace.

» Carry out honest and legible repairs using compatible materials.

» Fit new materials to the old rather than adapting the old to accept the new.

» Avoid artificially ageing new materials.

» Make additions reversible where possible and appropriate.

» Steer clear of conjecture and do not try to reinstate what has been lost.

» Undertake regular maintenance to avoid problems developing.

» Record and document.

» Retain the building and its fabric in its setting.

» Delay change until the full impact of what is intended is understood.

» Never be afraid of good new design where it complements the old.

Figure 3.06
New timber scarfed into a timber frame, ensuring only the most rotten material is lost.

'Being clear about the desired outcomes for each project is critical. It is vital to have an understanding and empathy with what a place needs from the outset and then to decide where to focus efforts and resources.'

Geoff Rich, Feilden Clegg Bradley Studios

Repair, don't restore

'Restoration' is a much used word but, for many who care about these structures, its use has specific and questionable connotations. In the strict architectural sense, 'restoration' means work intended to return a building or a component of a building to a perfect state or moment in time. This often leads to the unnecessary renewal of features that are worn, damaged or non-original, and the hypothetical reconstruction of missing elements, or indeed of an entire building. The outcome tends to be a reproduction, at the expense of genuine character, lacking both honesty and readability. In the words of William Morris, the result is '*a feeble and lifeless forgery*'; John Ruskin described restoration as '*a lie from beginning to end*'.

The favoured alternative is 'conservative repair'. This is central to good practice and does not mean that buildings can never be altered. It refers instead to an abstemious approach when carrying out work: doing as little as possible but as much as is necessary. This philosophy will ensure buildings with the maximum amount of their original fabric last as long as possible. As William Morris also said, it will see that we '*hand them down instructive and venerable to those that come after us*'.

While repair and conservation is forward-looking, restoration looks backwards because it is attempting to return the building to some real or imagined state in its past. Frequently this results in conjecture, as historic evidence is often lacking and modern materials, training and techniques can only produce a form of fakery intended to deceive the eye. Repair is about mending with minimum intervention and means that character and authenticity is retained with new work complementary but clearly visible. This is not to say that historic fabric should never be lost or altered. For example, past detailing might be badly executed and so permit water penetration, or loadings may have been poorly considered, resulting in stress on other elements of the building. More difficult is the decision, hopefully rare, to sacrifice fabric to accommodate change in order to make the building viable in the future. What must not happen is for any of these factors to be used as an excuse to destroy original fabric unnecessarily.

Astley Castle is a good example of difficult decisions that sometimes have to be made. The first phase of the project involved clearance and consolidation. The collapsed masonry and timbers had to be cleared from inside the ruin and the walls then had to be pieced back together and stabilised. As spaces were cleared, areas could be properly surveyed and assessed for the first time. A ten-year-old survey drawing of the original building gave some idea of how elements of the structure may have looked and there was some discussion about reinstating certain elements,

Figure 3.07
Retaining old material through careful repair to timber doors .

including window mullions and chimney stacks, but the team reached a position relatively quickly where they decided against reconstruction due to the difficulties of guaranteeing authenticity as well as economic constraints. The debate included conservation bodies and the Landmark Trust (the client), and ranged from the macro-decisions about setting to detailed discussions about whether to apply lacquer to old joinery in order to delay its decay. Again, conservative repair parameters were applied and there was a conscious decision against fakery or introducing any element of pastiche.

Sympathetic re-use

Buildings have always been reused and reinvented. Long-term rather than temporary re-use is always preferable and informed judgements based on an understanding of the history of the building make for the best solution, although temporary uses can sometimes prevent demolition when no permanent use is immediately foreseeable.

Essential questions to ask include:

» What impact will re-use have in terms of loss of fabric?

» Will re-use result in the loss of historic machinery or fittings?

» Will re-use affect the scale of the building?

» How far can re-use be taken without losing the essence of the original?

» What are the community and social consequences of reusing the building?

» Will the elements of new design be 'of today'?

'We strive to come to an understanding of a place or building, its history and the reasons for the changes made to it. We see the part we play as fitting into a continuum, where we can make what is already architecturally rich more distinct by taking away the irrelevant but also adding – enhancing the historic by casting it in a new light. It's about looking at the building itself and establishing what is really terrific and how it works.'

Clare Wright, Wright & Wright Architects

ARCHITECTURAL CONTEXT

Bringing new design to the rural scene is often more challenging than in the urban environment. One well-received response is Ditchling Museum in East Sussex. Here, none of the existing buildings were particularly strong aesthetically; their interest lay in their generic quality and the way in which they had evolved, with each layer of evolution being of its time. The architecture is shaped as much by the context and external space as it is by the internal dynamic.

The approach taken at Ditching Museum represents a collage of different styles, something altogether of today and avoiding what would have been an easy and poor pastiche of roof tiles and timber. Despite this, the buildings echo the traditional Sussex vernacular, subtly manipulating its form and bringing it up to date through modern interpretation and a choice of materials that includes black zinc.

Figure 3.08
A rendering of Astley Castle in its ruinous state.

Figure 3.09
Different forms and materials integrated at Ditchling Museum, East Sussex (far left).

Figure 3.10
Victorian shapes and themes developed at St Pancras Hotel, London (left).

There is a much more obvious reference to the past at St Pancras Hotel, London, where in the new wing Richard Griffiths Architects has interpreted the work of Gilbert Scott with a degree of abstraction. The new work goes back to the material and geometric base but without the mouldings and extra layers of dressing that were applied to the original.

Proportion and hierarchy

New design must consider the surrounding scale, hierarchy and massing of existing buildings. Sometimes it is assumed that additions should be smaller and subservient to the original building but this is not necessarily the case. Subservience is not the only possible relationship between proportion and the massing of the built forms. The qualities that lead to a favourable outcome may be varied and even contradictory, based on a hierarchy of scale and materials, whether the structures are heavyweight or lightweight, look the same or are different.

The concrete architecture of the National Theatre contains the strong human presence of performers and audience but, in form, it is powerful with surface textures that, instead of being slick, are undeniably vivid.

'At Ditchling Museum we felt that the new structures should feel as if they had been inserted in the same semi ad hoc way as the earlier buildings, so they look almost casually placed. We like the idea that, if you catch sight of one building out of the corner of your eye, you would think it had been there forever, but there is also something that makes you look again and, as you look, you realise there are other things going on.'

Adam Richards, Adam Richards Architects

Figure 3.11
Converted and extended,
the Granary, seen across
Barking Creek.

This left Haworth Tompkins looking for an architectural language for its interventions that would be recognisably new but would avoid being too flimsy a contrast to the original. Many designers might instinctively have set something spidery and minimal against the National's massive structures so that it would be notionally invisible. For Haworth Tompkins this was seen to be a false step, as it would simply have appeared brittle and thin against a building that embodied so much personality and human texture. Consequently, the new work is visible and solid and every bit of its time as the original.

Mass need not be overpowering. At the nineteenth century Granary, on Barking Creek, Pollard Thomas Edwards added an extension to the brick building that creates a pair of 'non-identical twins', complementary and balanced in weight. The new building, completed in 2011, is respectful of the

proportions of the original, taking its cue from the strong gabled form of the early structure but exploiting a prismoidal form. Due to its steep pitch, one corner of the roof essentially becomes a wall that incorporates roof windows. The geometry is tricky. To achieve the desired effect required crisp detailing of the bronze cladding and window details, along with the challenge of how to deal with water run-off without having an evident gutter.

In some cases the proportions embraced in a new building pay homage to the old. This is so with the extension that Chris Dyson Architects designed at Wapping, east London, for an early nineteenth century, Grade II listed, end-of-terrace house. The openings on the 2014 extension allude to Georgian proportion and, subtly, to the local warehouse architecture while being in every way modern. The style is taken a stage further through the bronzed casement windows – rather than sashes – inserted into these openings.

Figure 3.12
Georgian styles
reimagined for a 2014
house extension in
Wapping.

Rhythm and juxtaposition

Accretions bring rhythm, subtlety, contrasts, clashes and shape to buildings. They have moulded our cities, towns and villages into the eclectic, characterful and sometimes disharmonious places they are today. They create new views and juxtapositions and introduce light, shade, variety, texture and interest, while representing layers of history that tell a story, so are hugely important in achieving a sense of place and context.

Figure 3.13
New walls and openings integrated into ruins at Astley Castle, Warwickshire.

In adding to old buildings, structure and atmosphere are important elements. The interdependence of old and new creates an interesting tension and a real challenge for new design is ensuring the credibility of the new structure while maintaining the presence of an old building that is known and loved.

An example of rhythm having being lost is the tendency during refurbishment within church and other similar interiors to 'join the dots' between columns and fill the spaces with a wall. This often leaves little or no differentiation between the old and new structures, while also preventing the building being revealed from different viewpoints.

Astley Castle shows that the possibilities offered by working with old buildings are much broader than might be imagined: the juxtaposition of the beautiful, old and patinated with the new, crisp and sharp can work to create spaces that are in tune with today. Much has to do with scale. With a ruin there is a danger that introducing scale and comfort might 'fight' the monumentality that can come with dilapidation and cause a loss of energy. It would be wrong to add complicated details and simply bring the ruin down to a domestic scale, so it is important to introduce items that temper the sense of the sublime. Instead, it requires rigour and an aesthetic that is tough and even brutal but, at the same time, feels habitable. Witherford Watson Mann formed compartments created by the primary and secondary structure, and windows were stepped back to form niches to provide a sense of depth to the walls.

Complementing or contrasting

How much should the 'wow factor' affect the thinking behind the designer's response when working in the historic environment? Competitions and the desire to impress a client means there is a pressure for a building to be photogenic or, more likely in the first instance, to look good as a computer-generated image (CGI). This is hardly a new phenomenon.

Figure 3.14
The City of London Information Centre – a bold design, but no threat to the mass of St Paul's Cathedral.

Throughout history, architects and builders have needed to impress and excite their clients. They have done so

Figure 3.15
The National Theatre
paint shop, matching the
original building in tone
but of different
construction and
materials.

both by complementing and contrasting with earlier structures, as well as in the settings of their new buildings.

In many cases, these structures work and should be applauded but they do require considerable thought in their execution and detailing: simply adding a glass box to a historic building is rarely the solution. Testament to the success of the bold, contrasting approach are structures like the City of London Information Centre, situated to the south-west of the south transept of St Paul's Cathedral. Despite having a dynamic and contemporary exuberance, this building, completed in 2007, does not impinge on key views of St Paul's but is impactful within the immediate area.

Such examples should not overshadow the quiet approach: buildings that complement and embrace the historic structures with which they are associated but without mimicking them.

Haworth Tompkins' work at the National Theatre embraces both genres alongside a good deal of best practice conservation in repairing the original structure. At one extreme, to the south of the theatre, it added a building to house the paint shop which is unmistakably new and where a very clear and early decision was taken that the addition could not and should not be an extension of Lasdun's architecture. It needed to read not only as a new object but as an object which was separated visually, as if it was a vessel moored alongside the old building.

As well as this unmistakably modern design, there are a number of different and much more subtle layers. Some are to do with reconfiguring and creating new spaces, others result from the need to conserve the original structure. These follow a more conservative approach, employing parts of Lasdun's material palette, and involve degrees of replacement and mending.

A complementary approach was brought to the National Theatre signage, which had been changed in the 1990s. Haworth Tompkins was keen to get as close as possible to the original, which it felt was part of the vision for the building as a whole, but this was impractical because the original work was not considered

sufficiently legible. Instead, the new signage is a very close copy – returning to the same sizing, the hierarchies of the signage strategy and the typeface – and simply changing the tone and shade.

These almost subliminal details may appear to be simple devices but it is important to acknowledge that they are not realised without an understanding of traditional as well as present-day methods and styles. Indeed, they sometimes mix architectural periods, materials and references to achieve

Figure 3.16
New signage at the
National Theatre, London,
developed from the
original typeface.

Figure 3.17
Modern functional
elements introduced to a
Lambeth Palace courtyard
provide character and
impact (far left).

Figure 3.18
The tower remnant of
Laughton Place, East
Sussex, with the 'ghosts' of
gables and openings (left).

complementary or contrasting effect. Used well, materials such as steel, glass and timber can act as the perfect foil to heavy masonry buildings. The glass roof introduced over a courtyard at Lambeth Palace, in London, in 2000, coupled with a steel-and-glass bridge that spans diagonally across the space below, provides both character and impact.

Loose fit

Sir Alexander John Gordon, in his role as President of the Royal Institute of British Architects, defined 'good architecture' in 1972 as buildings that exhibit '*long life, loose fit and low energy*' – the 3L Principle. This is an important concept to consider when thinking about the adaptation of old buildings and the benefits of adopting the principles of loose fit are particularly relevant.

Long life and low energy translate readily into today's language of sustainability and resilience but are not always put into practice. New homes have a notional lifespan of just 60 years, while many of the building products used within them have an even shorter life expectancy. At the same time, commercial and office buildings are sometimes built and demolished in a timeframe of as little as 20 years. This is far from sustainable and it is perplexing to consider that the older part of a building – perhaps 200 years old – might easily outlive a new extension. Long life and low energy (and low carbon) principles should apply to the design of all buildings, as well as consideration of its day-to-day use. Loose fit is a harder concept and not much seen today when everything is designed to a tight brief and a functional end purpose. Over-specification can result in a lack of flexibility and designs that are not themselves open to further development. To embrace loose fit, this mindset needs to shift: a room is just a room and can, in many buildings, be purposed in numerous ways: sitting room, bedroom, study, office, showroom, shop, gallery.

GUARDING A LEGACY

The value of old buildings is deeper than their bricks and mortar. They are special because of those hard-to-define qualities of character and atmosphere: the ghosts of history, textural layers laid down not only by the original builders and craftspeople but by those who have inhabited the structure and that intangible feeling of a place steeped in memories. These attributes are very easily marred and cannot be imitated or recreated. Old buildings mature and gain integrity with time and, as they age, the bond with their site strengthens.

Readability and honesty

Carefully considered workmanship does justice to old buildings, leaving the most durable and useful record of what has been done. On the other hand, work concealed deliberately or artificially aged, even with the best intentions, is likely to mislead. To be able to 'read' a building is to understand its history and its development. Surface clues may, for example, reveal, through an indentation or outline, where once there was a window or door opening. Similarly, new wood may be spliced to old where the original timber has been lost or weakened by rot or beetle attack.

Legibility need not result in repairs or alterations that are ugly. Many old buildings have gained their charm and character from the patching and piecing in of new sections that are clearly different from the original fabric. It is not unusual for craftsmen to discreetly date their work for future reference. There is no justifiable reason why modern additions should not add equal character and understanding, although achieving readability when making changes or additions to a new building inevitably demands care, thought and determination. Good new design and carefully selected materials need not obscure readability and should provide an honesty that is refreshing and attractive while avoiding unnecessary technical complexity in construction or technique. In achieving this, technical compatibility between the new and old materials is essential to prevent deterioration or failure of the building's fabric and structure.

In the past, materials have frequently been salvaged from older structures for re-use but this is not always wise. The practice confuses the history, understanding and appreciation of a building while potentially adding an element of fakery. Trading and recycling architectural materials, while appearing 'green', has also been known to encourage architectural theft. From a durability perspective, the performance of these materials cannot always be predicted. For example, old bricks might be unsuitable for external works if previously used internally, and clay roof tiles may be reaching the end of their life so will fail at an early date due to inherent frost damage. On the other hand, using new traditional materials, such as peg tiles and handmade bricks, helps sustain their production and provides employment, keeping traditional skills and manufacturing alive. Alongside this comes an honesty in materials and craftsmanship.

This places an emphasis on making something that has been beautifully tailored. It is a way of thinking being adopted in other areas of life such as 'real' campaigns and the move towards 'slow' foods and handmade goods. Some might see

> '**The way we perceive buildings isn't solely an architectural thing. We don't just appreciate them, we experience them and therefore all of the extraneous matter – the landscape, the things around them, the context – actually has an impact on how we perceive the architecture itself. It's very, very hard just to have a purely narrowly architectural response to something.**'
>
> **Paddy Dillon, Haworth Tompkins**

Figure 3.19
Handmade bricks being dried, prior to firing.

this as venturing back to the Arts and Crafts ideals of William Morris, although the movement now is forward-looking and there is little emphasis on nostalgia.

Clear evidence of readability exists in the conversion of the 1808 Martello Tower Y on the Suffolk coast by Piercy&Company. Here, despite the roof extension having a congruency between the contemporary and historic, the two elements are distinctly different both externally and internally. There is no doubt that the undulating roof that has been added to this scheduled monument is very much of today as it appears to hover above the early nineteenth century brickwork below.

Trickier, and greatly debated, is what to do when, say, the heart of a Georgian terrace is destroyed by explosion or fire. Should this be rebuilt in a bold, current style or in replication of the earlier classical style? There are plenty of examples of poor work resulting from the filling of these gaps after bombing in the Second World War. Cases such as these and, indeed, where interiors have been damaged beyond simple repair, are likely to demand a variety of different approaches.

Figure 3.20
A pair of new houses provides a well-mannered inclusion in a London Edwardian terraced street (left).

The one common thread is that, whatever the intended solution, it should require the highest quality of design and craftsmanship. How strong the continuum and likenesses are depends upon the element being considered: materials, construction or aesthetics.

Figure 3.21
The form of the Dovecote, at Snape Maltings, Suffolk, reimagined in Cor-Ten steel (below).

Figure 3.22
The Ikon Gallery,
Birmingham, with new
insertions and a rebuilt
tower.

'We see buildings as living
organisms with a series of layers
and inevitably adaptions over a
course of life, there to be
celebrated and to be physical.'

Tom Bloxham, Urban Spash

Even where the aesthetics are replicated and the materials are matched exactly, the construction techniques hidden from view may of necessity be of today to meet regulatory and cost constraints.

A pair of infill houses in London by Knox Bhavan illustrates the way new design may be assimilated into an Edwardian terrace without disrupting the rhythm of the street typology. The building, completed in 2015, is readably and honesty new, with the front elevation composed of terracotta sandstone laid in ashlar courses with white sandstone lintels, columns and sills aligning with the stucco bands on the neighbouring houses.

Readability and honesty are factors that contribute to the success of the Dovecote Studio, which stands within the internationally renowned music campus at Snape Maltings on the Suffolk coast. The Victorian building collapsed in a storm in the 1970s. One option was to rebuild it in its original form but it was felt that this would destroy the building's romance and was not appropriate for a place where people come to hear contemporary music. Instead, Haworth Tompkins persuaded the clients to leave the structure as a ruin.

This generated the idea that an artist's studio could be dropped in, so rather than being built on its walls, the new Cor-Ten steel structure uses the ruin as a socket and sits within it. This mirrors the roof shape of the original dovecote and has the same hue as the reddish orange local brick of the surrounding buildings. Seen across the marshes on a misty morning, this almost gives the illusion that the old dovecote has suddenly, magically come back to life. Moving closer, there is the realisation that it is actually a far more enigmatic and recent object. Internally, the walls and ceiling of the space are lined with spruce plywood, while a large north-light roof window provides even light. A small writing platform inside offers visiting composers, writers and visual artists views of the neighbouring marshes.

A somewhat different, and possibly contentious, approach was taken by Levitt Bernstein in the creation of the Ikon Gallery in Birmingham, completed in 1997. Here the old school building had been gutted by fire, so little of the interior remained. Also lost was the clock tower, which had been a landmark in the area. The reinstatement of this feature was seen as essential to the scheme, and to Birmingham's Brindleyplace redevelopment area, where the old school building embodies strong links to the past.

Many would regard this as smacking of restoration but there are counter-arguments. Visually the tower is significant and, without it, the essence of the building's overall composition and focus would have been devalued, with the building itself losing gravitas within Brindleyplace. The reinstatement of the tower – now part of the building's energy strategy – creates a striking juxtaposition, with the contrasting materials and detailing of the new extensions highlighting the aesthetic qualities of both new and old architecture. Extensive photographs and drawings existed, so the new tower was a re-creation, rather than a re-invention, and the decision to rebuild it was backed by both the conservation officer and local people.

Reversibility

Buildings rarely remain unchanged but conservation philosophy looks for reversibility in alterations based on the premise that interventions can potentially be later removed without any discernible harm having been done to the original fabric. This thinking is embraced in the Burra Charter, which states: '*Reversible changes should be considered temporary. Non-reversible change should only be used as a last resort and should not prevent future conservation action.*'

This premise has its roots in the fact that today's interventions are responding to current needs so may play a role in only a comparatively short part of the buildings history and that future generations should have an opportunity to understand anew the historic significance of the building's fabric. Two other strands emerge from this argument. Firstly, embracing this philosophy is a way of further strengthening conservation principles. Secondly, it may enable changes to a building that would otherwise be deemed too damaging if reversibility was not a prerequisite of the proposed scheme.

Facadism

To leave the two-dimensional facade of a building and strip away all that lies behind it is hardly honest but, in recent decades, this is often how historic buildings have been 'retained' in the face of development that looks to maximise square metreage. This process of facadism creates monuments to history reminiscent of a Hollywood backlot, allowing the space left by the demolition of the major part of the old building to be built upon at will.

Figure 3.23
A retained high-street facade in Oxford Street, London, braced in position while excavations continue behind (far left).

Figure 3.24
The facade of Sir Thomas Edwin Cooper's 1925 Lloyd's building in the City of London (left).

Facadism lacks truth. It allows the marketing of homes or commercial spaces that retain a vestige of history, and which may still contribute to place-making, but what is left has no structural or design integrity. Step from the street through the facade and there is no authenticity, no relationship between old and new, no store of memories. Even more extreme are those examples where facades have been retained as a gesture to conservation planning but where the new building behind is highly visible and stands out in stark contrast. Arguably this approach is more honest, but the reminder of what has been abandoned and deleted is all the more acute.

JUNCTIONS

The junction between the old and the new can present significant challenges. Getting these points of transition right is vital to the success of a project not only ergonomically and aesthetically, but in the treatment of the historic fabric of the original. Although just a line on an architectural drawing, junctions must be considered technically and aesthetically and in some cases are designed to avoid all contact between the old and the new fabric. If not carefully thought through, they have the potential to be a visual disaster, a constructional nightmare and a long-term maintenance headache. From an aesthetic perspective

it is worth remembering that, in the past, accretions tended to be organic so little thought was generally given to punctuating the point where new met old. In all likelihood the change would be revealed simply through the natural use of different materials or building techniques driven by expediency rather than design.

At their simplest, junctions are a buffer between two buildings and may be hidden or camouflaged. Alternatively they can be revealed as a scene, legible both as a fully integrated

Figure 3.25
Junctions between different periods of building at the Tower of London.

Figure 3.26
The Bridge of Aspiration, the practical and symbolic link between the Royal Ballet School and the Royal Opera House, Covent Garden.

component of the buildings they link and as independent and eye-catching architectural elements in their own right. This is the case with the 2003 Bridge of Aspiration, high above Floral Street in London's Covent Garden, so named because it is crossed by upcoming young dancers on their way from the Royal Ballet School to the Grade I listed Royal Opera House.

Technical, philosophical and aesthetic considerations all come into play when designing junctions between old and new structures. The process can be tricky and frequently requires a diversity of skills: visual design, engineering, craftsmanship and a thorough understanding of materials. Junctions may be required to accommodate structural loadings and movement while preventing water ingress and providing airtightness. The approach will depend on scale and visibility; whether the addition is alongside, elevated or below; the layering of materials; the loadings that will be imposed; and whether there is an environmental change from one side of the junction to the other. The latter may relate to heat, humidity or a requirement for a higher or lower number of air changes and can be particularly relevant when moving from an older building to a new 'airtight' structure.

Figure 3.27
The new scheme at Chedworth, in the Cotswolds, including a viewing platform, sits directly on sound Roman walls.

Figure 3.28
The relationship of different materials at Astley Castle, Warwickshire.

Among the most unusual and understated junctions is at Chedworth Roman Villa in the Cotswolds. Here there was a need to protect mosaics and provide public access at this Scheduled Ancient Monument set within an Area of Outstanding Natural Beauty. Timber was chosen as it provided as lightweight a solution as possible, bearing straight onto the Roman sleeper walls below without requiring fixings into the masonry of the villa. This was felt to provide a more appropriate presentation than wrapping a building right over the top or building a structure inside and creating an 'umbrella' that went over the ancient walls. To form the junction, the Roman sleeper walls were minimally tidied up and topped with a timber sole plate which forms the base of the new structure. Partitions within the shelter are suspended, as are the walkways that enable visitors to get close to the mosaics.

Equally precious was the fragile existing structure at Astley Castle. This first had to be stabilised and the creation of junctions between old and new needed to be carefully understood and executed. During this process it would have been easy to tidy the original fabric of the walls in order to line up the new brickwork and make the job easier but, wherever possible, this was avoided and the team set themselves the rule of working with the fabric as found. The work required a multidisciplinary approach. Precast concrete beams were used, along with new brick, to bind the structure together. Throughout the project, Witherford Watson Mann and structural engineers Price & Myers worked to sensible rules of thumb: concrete never touches stone; precast concrete always bears on a brick pier, in turn bonded into the stone; clay is always used with clay; backfilling is with light aggregate; lime mortar is employed throughout.

A particularly difficult set of junctions was addressed by Donald Insall Associates during the design of the Copper Kingdom Centre, built on the site of the listed copper ore bins in Amlwch Port, Anglesey, north Wales. A suite of details was produced describing how the building would meet the rock face that forms the back wall of the site without losing the integrity of the various elements. Finding solutions was made more challenging as water naturally seeps from and runs down the rock face.

Externally, the architect worked closely with the copper installer to devise details for weatherproofing the junctions between the walls and the rock face and between the copper cladding and the rock face, as no industry guidelines existed. Most junctions were made by installing copper flashings into hand-cut rebates carefully chased into the rock face and walls; these were then packed with lime mortar pointing. Internally no flashings or other additions were introduced. Water penetration within the building is accepted by the client as a feature of the rock face. Critically, the mezzanine, flooring and other new elements have been kept around 300 mm away from the rock so there is never any direct contact between internal fabric and external walls.

This was challenging: channels had to be created to ensure water drains away from the interfaces between structural steelwork and the rock. A French drain (a discreet soakaway) was installed along the entire length of the base of the rock face to remove water.

'We realised our interventions between the new and the existing buildings would be absolutely key to making the building work. The basic philosophy when connecting the two was to have as light a touch as possible and to use an exiting doorway, or a window turned into a doorway, wherever we could; we didn't really make any new openings.'

John McElgunn, Rogers Stirk Harbour + Partners

Spaces and voids

Introducing a gap, or at least the feeling of space, between old and new structures may in some cases be an aesthetic device but more often is employed to avoid fixings or loading that would damage the

Figure 3.29
The Copper Kingdom Centre, where new work joins bare rock as well as the older building.

Figure 3.30
Foyer at Victoria Hall, Stoke-on-Trent, where old and new elements connect (far left).

Figure 3.31
A ground-level junction at the British Museum, where landscaping and building meet (left).

original building. In the case of Levitt Bernstein's scheme for Victoria Hall, in Stoke-on-Trent, the technique was employed twice. The slender bridges traversing the new four-storey atrium foyer between the Grade II listed assembly hall and the striking new building were cantilevered off columns in the new facility and joined only for stability to the original hall, but not taking any support from it. The new barrel-vault roof, which provides top lighting to the new foyer, sits similarly lightly on the old structure. Sealed at the junction against the weather, it barely touches but provides the illusion of unity.

When designing the British Museum's World Conservation and Exhibitions Centre in London, Rogers Stirk Harbour + Partners linked with the old museum in 16 places to provide access between the two buildings. In all cases the priority was to minimise damage to the original fabric, make necessary interventions reversible and accommodate movement between the structures. To achieve this, 'soft' joints were used and the weight of the bridges and other devices involved in creating the linkways was supported from the new building. Landscaping never touches the old museum buildings. Gaps of around 300 mm have been introduced at the boundaries to accommodate steel trays that hold small stones.

Glass slots

A glazed link, often in the form of a glass slot, is frequently seen as the acceptable form of junction and separation between old and new, and is the orthodoxy with many planning departments when a modern form is being placed next to a historic building. Many now regard this as something of a cliché and there is a shift away from this device as a default towards something quieter and more anonymous. Where glazing is seen to provide an answer, the qualities of the material must be considered. In plans and presentations, even in CGI visualisations, glass is often shown as if it were invisible and non-reflective, which can be at odds with the end result. The transparent nature of glass may pose issues of privacy for the building's occupants; light pollution may be a problem, especially in rural areas at night; and reflections both internally and externally are not always predictable.

Figure 3.32
Glass slot between old and new at the Grade I listed Cardigan Castle, Wales.

Shadow gaps

Figure 3.33
A discreet metal-panelled link between buildings at Ditchling Museum, East Sussex.

A 'quiet' way of achieving a junction is with indentations or shadow gaps within the structure. This device has been used at Ditchling Museum, where, instead of glazed panels, wide shadow gaps are formed in the black zinc. The concept means that, from the outside, the eye sees the listed cart lodge and the new tiled pavilion building rather than the junction. Inside, the space around the junction feels clean and uncluttered creating a sense of movement through it.

Changes of level

Steps and slopes provide a practical transition from one level to another but may also denote a conscious junction between old and new. This is often of necessity due to unavoidable changes in floor or ceiling height. The design for the Bridge of Aspiration responded directly to the fact that the openings it was linking were not in alignment either in plan or section. A conventional bridge with regular rectangular glass would have had uncomfortable junctions. As a result, a concertina of 23 square portals with glazed intervals was developed, supported from an aluminium spine beam. These rotate in sequence for the skew in alignment, performing a quarter-turn overall along the length of the bridge.

Even slight changes of level necessitated by technical considerations relating to junctions need careful consideration to prevent them becoming a trip hazard or creating an unacceptable bump. The latter is particularly relevant in museum or research environments where vibration to trolleys or apparatus passing over the junction is a concern, for example when delicate specimens or artefacts are being transported, such as at the British Museum's World Conservation and Exhibitions Centre.

Figure 3.34
The Bridge of Aspiration's elegant form, derived from complex mathematics and engineering (right).

Figure 3.35
One of the links between the British Museum and the World Conservation and Exhibitions Centre (far right).

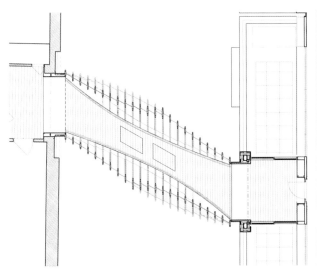

Structural loads

Inevitably, any addition is likely, at some point, to place a load on or near existing fabric. While this is primarily an engineering concern, the implications of accommodating the load can directly affect the outcome of a scheme aesthetically. This was the case at the Garden Museum, within the medieval and Victorian church of St Mary-at-Lambeth in London, where it was discovered that much of the church floor had little ability to support significant additional loading. Furthermore, a combination of archaeological constraints relating to excavating the floor and lack of funds to undertake archaeology or to pile meant that an innovative approach was required.

Investigation revealed that, beneath the oak floor, the nave columns stand on a brick wall that joins all of the columns running along the nave. Calculations established that, as long as the new CLT (cross-laminated timber) structure 'landed' within a 200 mm zone around the base of a column, the forces would successfully be transferred to the wall. Consequently, the building's existing geometry informed the new design, governing how the building is organised and how people circulate within it.

Compatibility and differential movement

New buildings can rarely be constructed in exactly the same way as older ones due to the demands of comfort, practicality, regulations, materials and building techniques. This means that consideration must be given to the compatibility of the different approaches to avoid the performance of the original fabric being compromised by the addition. In producing a specification it may be necessary to detail separate clauses for the existing and new buildings in terms of workmanship and materials.

Figure 3.36
The house in Wapping, with its end-of-terrace extension.

Another factor is that the foundations of a new building are likely to be deeper than the relatively shallow footings generally found beneath older buildings, so care must be taken to ensure that any differential settlement can be accommodated at the junction between the two. It should be remembered that most old buildings have settled long ago so further movement tends to be limited unless ground conditions or loadings change.

'Design tends to be the most successful when it's simple and straightforward and you don't design yourself a problem that then needs a maintenance procedure.'

Liz Smith, Purcell

Concerns over differential movement were addressed at Astley Castle by allowing the new brick to bear directly on the old stonework with no new foundations. This was based on the logic that the new walls are no higher than the original walls and are hollow, so compared with the historic dead weight, are lighter, even with a massive concrete lintel bearing on them.

In the case of the house at Wapping, the ground slab and foundations needed for the addition were substantial due to poor ground conditions. A fibrous board material housed in a recess faced with lime mortar creates a vertical movement joint while the old and new structures are linked with stainless steel ties designed to allow for some degree of flexibility.

Ventilation is equally important and must be maintained, for example in the void under original suspended timber floors. This is a common problem in extensions to terraced houses where air bricks are sealed when a solid floor is laid in the new addition, resulting in the cross-ventilation to the existing sub floor void being seriously compromised. Where this is unavoidable an alternative ventilation strategy should be included in the scheme.

DESIGNING FOR MAINTENANCE

Future maintenance is sometimes not sufficiently considered when making additions to older buildings, so detailing to design out maintenance needs, particularly at junctions, is vital. One of the most basic mistakes is when a single-storey rear extension is added to a house and the problem of how access is to be gained to clean, maintain and decorate the existing upper-storey windows and gutters is not considered. Such design oversights can result in substantial difficulties and costs, with the result that regular and proper maintenance is neglected.

Figure 3.37
Traditional materials can improve with age and acquire a new beauty.

Choice of materials may also affect future maintenance. Many modern materials need to look sharp and fresh but are not always visually forgiving if poorly maintained and will quickly appear shabby due to weathering, staining or scuffing. Conversely, traditional lime renders, plasters and limewashes generally retain a pleasing appearance even when neglected and frequently mature with age.

CHAPTER 4:
MATERIAL FACTS

Materials are at the heart of what makes old buildings special, so an appreciation of their attributes, coupled with careful choice, is essential for good design in historic environments. Alongside the beauty of the old, the qualities of modern materials should not be underestimated in creating sympathetic and dynamic schemes.

Construction methods and materials provide a primary source from which ideas and meaning can be drawn. They reflect people's tastes, skills and relationship with a locality while being imbued with beauty and character derived from texture, colour and the patina and blemishes of age and use.

Compatible traditional and natural materials, and the skills associated with them, inevitably have a big part to play in work associated with old buildings and in any project that seeks to improve the sustainability credentials of a scheme. The thoughtful use of materials provides the opportunity for a clearly identifiable non-historicist approach and there is a chance to be bold and creative without being disrespectful to the historic environment.

Figure 4.00
Door to the crypt at Christchurch, Spitalfields, London (left).

Figure 4.01
Corrugated and flat Cor-Ten steel used at the Gasworks, Gloucestershire, echoing agricultural forms (right).

While the values of traditional materials and techniques are key to the repair and renovation of old buildings, carefully selected alternatives will make sense in some situations and can clearly help to distinguish interventions from the surrounding existing elements. Even so, it is important not to choose materials simply because they are different from the original; differentiation is more subtle than this and should be based on reason and context.

Choice is made more difficult due to the vast palette of materials now available. Any new material should be looked at carefully, particularly if it appears to offer an easy solution to a problem. While traditional materials have a proven track record, not all modern materials are clearly understood and the process of ageing and issues of compatibility may not be fully appreciated. Much more is expected of buildings in performance terms than ever before and there is a danger of over-complication that can have an impact on historic fabric and the sustainability of the building.

'Buildings represent the cultural record of our life and so we have to assess their social, ecclesiastical and wider significance. Those values might override materials but materials must always serve the cultural philosophy of the building.'

Julian Harrap, Julian Harrap Architects

TRADITIONAL AND VERNACULAR BUILDINGS

Many old buildings had no architect in the sense that the term is understood today. Most vernacular buildings were built by local craftspeople, larger buildings by stonemasons and carpenters who took the role of master builder. They were familiar with the materials available to them and followed traditions handed down through generations.

Before the coming of the railways, moving materials over long distances was difficult and expensive, so builders exploited the materials that were immediately available in the surrounding landscape and underlying geology. As a result, a rich diversity of vernacular building styles developed across the UK, creating distinctive regional variations.

One of the most adaptable materials for building is wood and it was once plentiful in many parts of Britain. Buildings were framed in timber and jointed together with wooden pegs. Infill panels of wattle and daub or other materials were then inserted into the spaces, usually followed by coats of lime render and limewash. These buildings were roofed with thatch, often of locally sourced straw or reed, and later stone or clay tiles. Some places saw earth employed to construct the walls of buildings with techniques variously known as cob, clay lump, clay bat and rammed earth.

Figure 4.02
A Sussex cottage built of local iron-rich sandstone.

Clay has been fired to make bricks and tiles and these came to dominate many areas. In the stone-bearing regions, quarried stone is generally the main building material in the form of limestones, sandstones and granites, which occur in a great variety of colours and qualities. In addition, flint, pebbles, cobbles, slate and even chalk were used. For the builder, each offers different characteristics with some easily cut and shaped while others are much harder and remarkably resistant to weathering.

'In terms of the materials that we used at Ditchling Museum we wanted them all to be authentic and that you had a sense of their materiality whether you were looking at them, touching them or smelling them.'

Adam Richards, Adam Richards Architects

THE NEED TO BREATHE

Buildings constructed before around 1919 often perform differently to modern buildings. Many have solid walls of brick or stone which allow a degree of moisture penetration into their structure but damp problems are avoided due to the 'breathable' nature of the materials used, including weak and permeable mortars, plasters and renders based on lime, or sometimes earth or clay, and finishes such as limewash. While these materials absorb moisture, they also allow for easy evaporation. The water vapour is dispersed externally due to the drying effect of the wind and the sun, and internally as the result of air entering through gaps in the building fabric and the traditional use of large open fires that further promote air movement. In Scotland, the solid stone masonry often incorporates an airspace behind lath and plasterwork on the wall's internal face.

Providing that buildings constructed in this way are properly maintained, they remain essentially dry and in equilibrium and, even though some of the materials are relatively soft, their walls can endure for centuries even if in direct contact with the soil. Conversely, modern building construction relies on excluding water through the standard use of damp-proof courses, cavity walls and impermeable surfaces and membranes.

Both approaches have their place, but the use of modern products, such as cement-based materials, 'plastic' paints and waterproof sealants on buildings that were designed to be breathable inevitably proves disastrous. Cementitious mortars and renders are particularly damaging as they are hard and brittle and trap moisture. In the case of brickwork repointed with cement mortar instead of lime, the moisture typically moves to the face of the brick instead of escaping through the original, softer lime joints. The action of frost causes it to freeze and the brick's surface blows apart or 'spalls'.

Elsewhere, trapped moisture similarly causes surfaces to break down as damp patches and mould appear and rot and beetle infestation occurs.

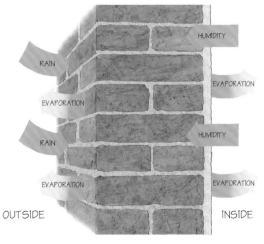

Figure 4.03
Breathability in a traditionally constructed solid wall.

This is likely to be harmful not only to the wellbeing of the building but also to its occupants.

Claims of breathability should be carefully examined. Many materials are breathable to some degree but a great many are not nearly breathable enough to be compatible with older buildings. As a rough guide, breathable materials that could be considered suitable for use should have a vapour resistance of no more than 2.5 MNs/g. In the case of multilayered materials, the vapour resistance of all layers together, including adhesives, must be calculated.

Figure 4.04
Spalling to the face of bricks resulting from cementitious repointing.

Breathability and air leakage

When working with old buildings, particularly when considering energy efficiency, it is essential not to confuse breathability with air leakage.

Breathability is the water vapour transmission rate, or the speed at which vapour permeates through a particular material or construction. Other important aspects of breathability relate to the material's hygroscopicity (ability to absorb or release water vapour) and capillarity (wicking action). Waterproof membranes and inappropriate materials, such as cement-based products, sealants and modern 'plastic' paints, all prevent traditional building fabric from breathing.

Air leakage or air permeability is not the same as breathability. It is uncontrolled draughts through joints and gaps in a building's fabric. It is perfectly possible to construct an airtight building that is still breathable.

Thermal insulation

Some modern insulation materials have the potential to trap moisture. In old buildings, this can cause problems such as interstitial condensation and mould growth, with consequential decay of the building fabric and poor indoor air quality.

Conversely, natural insulation materials are generally breathable and will act as moisture buffers, absorbing and releasing water as the relative humidity within the building increases or decreases. They are equally suitable for use in old and new buildings and add to the sustainability credentials of a scheme due to their low embodied carbon, the ability for plant-based materials to sequester CO_2 during growth, their recyclability at end of life and improvements to indoor air quality due to the fact that mould is not given conditions for growth and off-gassing tends to be negligible.

Figure 4.05
Forms of breathable insulation materials. Clockwise from bottom left: cellulose, wood fibre, hemp, aerogel, calcium silicate, jute, sheep's wool, foamed glass, clay, cork, and wood chip.

Numerous forms of natural insulation material are available, including wood fibre, jute, hemp, sheep's wool, cork and cellulose (recycled newspaper) products. Each has characteristics which help to create a healthy, comfortable, energy efficient and durable construction. Wood fibre insulation products alone offer solutions for roofs, floors and walls. These include flexible and rigid insulation boards, air-injected insulation as well as complete insulation systems.

In design terms, the down side of natural products can be that a greater thickness of material is required to achieve the same level of thermal performance compared with petrochemical and some mineral and composite products.

LIME

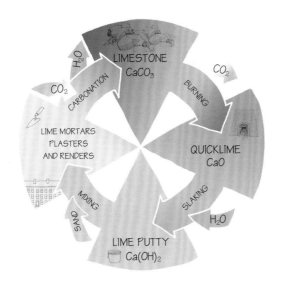

Figure 4.06
The lime cycle starts with limestone and returns to the same chemical composition.

Used for thousands of years, lime forms the basis of mortars, renders, plasters and paints and is a key component of most old buildings. It is essential to their repair and renovation and is available commercially in many forms for different applications, as natural hydraulic lime, lime putty or pre-mixed with aggregates. The material also has a growing role in new buildings, with a number of design benefits, and is being employed as a component of low-carbon, sustainable construction systems. Lime is a calcium-rich natural material produced by firing limestone (calcium carbonate) in a kiln, a process that drives off carbon dioxide. Non-hydraulic lime is made by slaking the resulting quicklime with water to create a slurry known as lime putty. By mixing this with sand or other aggregates, lime mortars, plasters and renders are made. As the lime sets in the air, carbon dioxide is re-absorbed and it returns to its original chemical form.

Incredibly versatile, lime has been described as the Gore-tex of the building world as it allows water vapour to escape from a structure rather than trapping it. Lime has many other properties. With wonderful, soft-looking textures, lime weathers gracefully and, in the form of limewash, can add striking colour and beauty to buildings. In construction terms, lime offers flexibility and has the ability to self-heal so allows a degree of movement, saving the need for regular expansion joints. This has the design benefit of allowing large uninterrupted expanses of masonry.

Figure 4.07
The appearance of this limewashed Welsh farmhouse changes with the weather conditions.

From a sustainability perspective, when a building is demolished lime mortar can easily be removed from bricks or stones, enabling their re-use. When working with lime there is less waste than with cement mortars as mixes can remain useable the following day and some may be stored for months or even years under the right conditions.

Lime mortars

Mortar joints account for at least 17 per cent of the surface area of brickwork so the colour and texture of the mortar and the style of pointing will dramatically change a wall's appearance and mortar mixes must be carefully considered. At the Dovecote Studio, at Snape Maltings in Suffolk, the original lime for the brick mortar was burnt locally so has small specks of chalk in it and, where new work was undertaken, this was reproduced as closely as possible. Historically a number of techniques were used to enhance the appearance of mortar joints. Galleting, the technique of pushing small stones into the mortar before it set, was employed in both brick and stone work to pack out wide joints and to provide a decorative effect.

Lime renders

The facades on many buildings have a plain render finish but it is useful to appreciate variants in local tradition. For example, roughcast, known in Scotland and northern England as 'harling', is a lime render mixed with pea gravel thrown onto the face of the wall. It is commonly used in exposed locations as its increased surface area serves to maximise evaporation and protects the underlying wall material against driving rain.

Limewash

Used since early times, limewash is an attractive and breathable finish for external and internal walls. Made simply by blending lime putty with water, and available ready-made, it has a matt finish and can be coloured with pigments. It is ideal for porous surfaces, such as brick, stone, lime plaster or roughcast, and, when used externally, typically needs renewing about every five years, although in previous times limewashing was part of the annual routine maintenance of houses, farm buildings and many rural churches.

Limecrete

Sometimes known as lime concrete, limecrete is a concrete where lime is used instead of cement. Should it be necessary to replace a concrete floor that has been added to an old building, and is trapping moisture, a limecrete floor offers a viable alternative as it is capable of providing a structural floor slab that is vapour permeable, includes insulation and can accommodate underfloor heating. Limecrete floors are being installed in increasing numbers into both old and new buildings. In the cart lodge at Ditchling Museum in East Sussex, which serves as a combined foyer, shop and café, the earth floor was replaced with a limecrete slab topped with slate flags. This helps the building to breathe – in the case of the cart lodge through the joints between the flags – in the way that it had done throughout its life.

Figure 4.08
Small stones or 'gallets' used to pack out mortar joints (far left).

Figure 4.09
Limecrete floors offer a breathable alternative to concrete (centre).

Figure 4.10
A hempcrete end gable wall of a barn conversion allows the original timber frame to breathe (right).

Hemp lime

Another non-traditional lime product is hemp lime or hempcrete. This mix of hemp – a natural plant fibre – with hydraulic lime and various additives offers excellent thermal insulation, thermal inertia and humidity control. Its uses range from providing insulation to the walls of medieval timber-framed houses to constructing extensions and new buildings; in its panellised form it has even been used to build superstores. Hemp lime allows the creation of buildings with the soft lines of traditional structures or a modernist aesthetic. It is this versatility, and the fact that it is a low-impact building material, that makes it particularly useful when designing new work in the historic environment.

CONSTRUCTION

Old buildings are generally much simpler, and have far fewer components than those constructed today, with their walls essentially formed of a solid homogeneous layer, perhaps finished with plaster or render. Today, layered construction is used, which creates a visual and functional distinction between the outside and inside, while sandwiching further unseen layers of insulation and vapour barriers. This means even the simplest wall will be multilayered and inherently complex. It reflects the move from traditional breathable construction to modern methods that are designed to keep moisture out, create a sealed building envelope and achieve highly energy-efficient buildings.

Increasingly, the layered approach is being applied to traditional buildings during retrofits where the need for energy efficiency measures means that insulation and membranes are being installed either internally or externally. Additionally, the design challenges associated with the installation of modern building services, ranging from ducting for ventilation to electrical cabling, means that service voids are necessary so internal linings are incorporated. All these measures can result in original plaster surfaces being hidden or destroyed and have implications for the potential spread of fire. From a building performance perspective they may also have the effect of trapping moisture, especially where walls are exposed to wind-driven rain, and separating the thermal mass of the building from the interior.

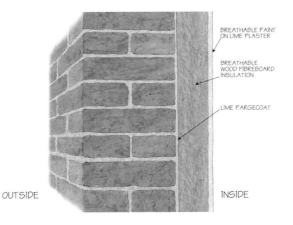

BREATHABLE PAINT ON LIME PLASTER

BREATHABLE WOOD FIBREBOARD INSULATION

LIME PARGECOAT

OUTSIDE   INSIDE

Figure 4.11
A breathable internal insulation layer added to a traditional solid wall.

UNDERSTANDING MATERIALS

Traditional materials, such as lime, timber, brick and stone, risk being seen as old-fashioned and unsuited to new design. In reality, they not only have the capacity to offer outstanding aesthetic qualities but come with a record of successful long-term performance and durability while, in most cases, addressing concerns around embodied carbon and sustainability.

Equally, modern materials bring new and exciting opportunities within the context of new work. The danger is they may be used by default when attempting to bring innovation to a scheme. With any work it should always be that the best material is used rather than a choice based on a preconceived idea.

The use of materials and building methods that are of equal or better quality to those used in the existing structure is always beneficial. Not only does quality enhance design, it ensures survival for future generations with good materials more likely to become part of the natural and graceful ageing of the building. It is worth remembering that, had new or better materials been

Figure 4.12
A concrete lintel being craned into place at Astley Castle, Warwickshire.

available, past generations would almost certainly have used them. This brings with it the realisation that, had they been capable of making glass without bubbles and ripples in the 18th and 19th centuries, the Georgians and Victorians would undoubtedly have used it and the faces of many old buildings would have been denied the beauty that comes with these imperfections.

In line with material trends, the building-related trades have subtly changed. While craftspeople still specialise within their individual disciplines using their own particular skills, they may integrate modern materials and methods to solve problems. For example, a carpenter might now use stainless steel nuts and bolts when repairing timbers or a bricklayer may use machine-made blocks but then use a craft skill to lay them out.

In the case of Astley Castle in Warwickshire, the new masonry work saw special hollow precast reinforced concrete lintels craned into place and glulam beams used where standard timber joists would have provided insufficient strength or span. When redeveloping Park Hill in Sheffield, Urban Splash used colourful anodised aluminium panels to echo the coloured brick tones of the original facade and emphasise the building's modular structure.

Figure 4.13
Park Hill, Sheffield, facade with new aluminium panels.

Colour and texture

For the designer, traditional, natural and handmade materials provide a rich palette of colours and textures but the juxtaposition of the old and the patinated with the new and the crisp is often hugely rewarding.

Colour is a notable feature of many old buildings and in some cases results from coatings of limewash pigmented with vibrant hues. A notable feature of limewash is its visual softness and its ability to reflect different moods, ever changing as it becomes wet or dry: dull and sombre when damp from a downpour but radiating life when dry and bathed in sun. The coating is sacrificial, so it gently wears away, but still has the ability to look beautiful, whereas modern masonry paints simply become tired and grubby.

Traditional exterior plasterwork is invariably slightly rough and irregular, and was sometimes indented or moulded with detail known as pargetting. Consequently, the surface has a depth accentuated by shadows as light moves across it.

At Ditchling Museum, Adam Richards Architects took the idea of shadows to a new level. Black zinc has been used as a cladding material to allow it to behave somewhat like a shadow, with the result that it disappears into the background.

The decision to use black zinc cladding was partly driven by budget, but there was also a rationale relating to the material palette. Black-stained timber is part of the local scene and, crucially, there is a house directly opposite the museum clad in black mathematical tiles that have a shimmering quality, like mussel shells.

'I'd like to think that the tradesmen who originally built Astley Castle would recognise the value of the new materials we've used and, at the same time, they'd say "I wish we'd had that!"'

William Mann, Witherford Watson Mann

Figure 4.14
Black zinc used as cladding at Ditchling Museum, East Sussex.

THE MATERIALS PALETTE

The five key materials – timber, clay, stone, metal and glass – provide the ingredients with which almost all architecture can be made to sing. Further versatility is now provided by concretes, new alloys and plastics. Within each material group the range of options available to the designer is extensive. Not only must the choice of the material 'family' be considered but also the colour, texture and even the size of the individual components. In addition, factors such as performance, durability and embodied carbon should be taken into account.

The new lavatory block at Layer Marney Tower in Colchester, Essex, perfectly illustrates how careful choice of materials may successfully express a look that is both harmonious and recognisably of today. Designed by Freeland Rees Roberts and completed in 2009, the linear building is constructed of the most traditional of material palettes: handmade bricks, with an oak frame supporting a lead roof. Along with the materials, some of the construction details echo the Tudor gatehouse, including the bond of the bricks.

Materials allow the designer to take some of the qualities of the existing building and re-imagine them in new work. The 2007 addition by Mole Architects to Ramblers, a listed stone cottage in Pulborough, West Sussex, does this through the use of green oak cladding to the walls and clay tiles on the roof. While the treatment of the old and new elevations is very different, the tonal and textural harmony is maintained.

Figure 4.15
The new lavatory block at Layer Marney Tower, Colchester.

A more obviously contemporary, although nonetheless harmonious, style was adopted by Rogers Stirk Harbour + Partners for the British Museum's World Conservation and Exhibitions Centre, completed in 2014. At the outset the materials used in surrounding buildings were analysed. The Bloomsbury area of London, in which the museum stands, is made up almost entirely of white Portland stone buildings or stock brick terraces. It became clear that the new extension should be part of the white, larger-scale institutional buildings rather than the smaller-scale domestic ones.

Instead of matching the Base Bed Portland stone of the neighbouring museum, which comes alive when sculpted for cornicing and other details, Portland stone from the Roach Bed was chosen as this looks good when used in flat panels. The stone contains holes left when the remains of fossilised turreted gastropods and clams were washed away and, even from a distance, clearly communicates through its materiality that it is natural stone and not synthetic.

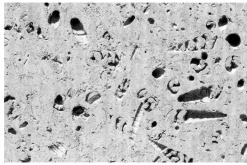

Figure 4.16
The 2014 World Conservation and Exhibitions Centre, to the right of the British Museum building (far left).

Figure 4.17
Roach Bed Portland stone used at the World Conservation and Exhibitions Centre, part of the British Museum (left).

Timber

Timber's versatility knows few bounds and, as well as being one of the most traditional and ubiquitous materials, it is viewed today as among the most sustainable and the only replenishable carbon-capturing structural building material. Coupled to this, technological innovation means it is suitable for almost any aspect of construction, whether structural or purely aesthetic. From a visual perspective, timber is often seen as a cladding material: timber weatherboarding first appeared on agricultural, vernacular and industrial buildings. Early cladding was of oak or elm but later softwood boards were used and it became more fashionable for domestic buildings in later Georgian times. Generally timber weatherboarding was laid horizontally; more commonly today the boards are fixed vertically and form part of a rainscreen that may include membranes and insulation materials.

Timber was the main component of the two-storey extension by James Gorst Architects at Wakelins, a Grade II listed Tudor farmhouse in Suffolk. When work started much of the timber frame of the existing house was beyond repair and new oak had to be inserted carefully. An extension was constructed alongside using prefabricated timber panels clad in oak. The form and materiality of the extension provides a clear visual contrast to the render of the building that it joins, helped by the deep rebate of the vertical cladding, which creates depth and character.

More subtle is the simple extension to the Grade I listed Holy Trinity Church at Goodramgate in York. Again, oak was used but it was finished with an adze to give a distinctive and recognisable texture, while the timber is expected to weather to a colour that increasingly matches the stone of the church.

The versatility of timber cladding as a design element is further illustrated by its use at Hunsett Mill, in Stalham, Norfolk. Here the design of a large addition to a nineteenth century mill keeper's house was guided by a focus on environmentally friendly practices and the desire to create a building that would sit easily beside the Grade II listed windmill within the protected landscape of the Norfolk Broads.

Designed by Acme, the extension, completed in 2010, echoes the pitched roofs and dark timber boards that are part of the traditional Broads vernacular. While the large volume of the extension could easily have been overpowering, it is instead a 'shadow' behind the existing red-brick cottage, an effect achieved through the use of charred cedar boards for the vertical cladding. This was sourced from Japan, where the use of charred timber (*yakisugi*) for building purposes is a common practice and where its production is more sustainable than in the UK. The treatment is not merely aesthetic but functional, weatherproofing and preserving the timber without the use of chemicals.

Behind the facade, the extension is constructed entirely of cross-laminated timber to form the load-bearing walls, floors and the distinctive saw-tooth roof. The timber was selected for its insulating and thermal

Figure 4.18
The oak-clad extension to Wakelins, Suffolk.

regulating properties, and was harvested from sustainable forests.

Timber is equally effective when employed internally. Communion Architects used local oak to clad the simple cube-shaped pod it created within the twelfth century St Andrew's Church in Herefordshire. A new suspended oak floor allowed the original floor of the Grade I listed church to remain undisturbed while allowing for a heating system to be installed underneath and level access to be provided to the entire building.

Figure 4.19
The extension at Holy Trinity Church, York, was finished in adze-textured oak boards.

Engineered timber

Embracing a range of products that are engineered to precise design and technical specifications, engineered timber allows imaginative schemes using timber boards, joists and beams that would have been impossible in the past. Among the most popular in this context is cross-laminated timber (CLT), which is strong and comparatively light.

Figure 4.20
Hunsett Mill, Norfolk, with an extension clad in charred timber.

At Ditchling Museum, Adam Richards Architects was keen to embrace the philosophy of the artists who came to the village at the tail end of the Arts and Crafts movement. One of the things that was important to them was truth to materials. CLT offered an opportunity to follow this ethos by leaving it visible within the building, with an oiled finish, to show material honesty. This allows visitors to see what the building is made of while offering benefits architecturally and spatially, giving large unobstructed volumes that other materials of comparable cost could not.

At the Garden Museum in Lambeth, the nature of the Grade II* listed church precluded anything touching the existing structure except for the floor. CLT has been used to make the staircase and a cantilevered entrance area. The only other suitable materials would have been steel or in situ concrete, both of which would have been too heavy to stand on the existing timber floor, and too expensive.

> '*Very often in our work the conceptual idea is related to a material or a way we will deal with a material and how that will then relate to the place. By using CLT we realised that we could achieve what we wanted because we'd found this material that we could just use in its out-of-the-factory form, we wouldn't need to paint it or treat it or do anything to it.*'
>
> **Alun Jones, Dow Jones Architects**

Clay

Like timber, clay is among the most traditional of all building materials and, before easy transport was available, it was frequently dug on or close to the site of a new building. As a consequence, the nature of local clays has resulted in a vast palette of grey, purple, buff and brown bricks and tiles that contribute much to regional identity.

Figure 4.21
New facilities within St Andrew's Church, Herefordshire (right).

Figure 4.22
CLT boards during construction at the Garden Museum, London (far right).

Bricks

Itinerant gangs of brickmakers once travelled from site to site handmaking bricks. These were generally longer, wider and shallower than modern examples but bricks have historically been sized to fit a man's hand, making them easy to handle. With mass production, bricks became more regular in shape, size and colour. More recently imperial brick sizes gave way to metric. The size of brick chosen influences the overall appearance of a facade, as does the bond or laying pattern. The new work at Astley Castle is clearly shown through the use of brick as a contrast to the original stone of the building. Instead of standard 65 mm bricks, 37 mm bricks were employed, enabling the lines of the irregular masonry to be followed more closely.

High-quality brickwork was often formed using specially made bricks called 'rubbers', which could be carved, shaped and then laid very accurately with extremely thin joints. This style is known as 'rubbed and gauged'. Imitating gauged work, 'tuck pointing' employs flush pointing that matches the colour of the bricks but a fine line is indented into the mortar and filled with a lime putty/silver sand mix to give the impression of a narrow joint.

Tiles

Clay roof tiles bring the same aesthetic qualities as brick and they frequently replaced thatch, particularly in towns and cities, due to their fire resistance. Early tiles were 'peg tiles', so called because they had one or two holes to accommodate small wooden pegs, and later nails, which hooked onto timber laths. During the nineteenth century projecting nibs were added to the top edge of tiles to fulfil the same function.

In some areas, pantiles are common. These have a distinctive 'S' shape designed to interlock with the neighbouring tile. This means that the tiles may be laid to a lower pitch so are ideal for lean-to extensions. Handmade roof tiles are of many different shades, shapes and finishes. Machine-made tiles began to be manufactured from the nineteenth century; these are smoother and more regular in size and shape than handmade products. In the Victorian era, roof decoration reached a peak with the use of multicoloured tiles and decorative ridges.

Faience

Since the late eighteenth and early nineteenth centuries, glazed clay has been popular, especially for commercial buildings.

Figure 4.23
Traditional handmade bricks showing a range of natural colour variations after firing.

Figure 4.24
Rubbed and gauged brickwork with fine lime mortar joints.

Figure 4.25
Handmade clay tiles at Ditchling Museum, East Sussex.

Figure 4.26
Faience used alongside glass at the Holburne Museum, Bath.

Faience was chosen for the fins that feature on the facade of the extension to the Holburne Museum in Bath due to its reflective qualities and also because it echoes the materials found in items displayed within. Each of the panels and fins was glazed by hand, with a base coat rich in manganese and copper applied first to produce a green-brown colour. A mottled pattern was then applied containing manganese and titanium oxide, which reacted with the base coat to form a distinctive blue-green pattern.

Stone

Stone is difficult and expensive to transport so, traditionally, quarrying was carried out as close as possible to a building under construction. As a result, local quarries were widespread. The diversity of geology across the UK means there are many stone types, giving rise to distinct vernacular styles and regional appearances, from flint walls in Sussex to fine sandstone in Edinburgh. Each type of stone has its own characteristics. Broadly speaking, sandstone tends to be difficult to carve and embellish, granite is incredibly durable but difficult to work, while limestone lends itself to shaping and fine detailing.

The construction of stone walls varies depending on the status of the building and the material available. Random rubble walls are common, built, as the name suggests, from variously sized unfinished stones. Coursed rubble walls are laid in distinct lines with stones that are sometimes squared. The finest 'ashlar' work comprises blocks of dressed stone laid in even courses with almost invisible joints between them.

In the City of London, Bracken House was constructed in the second half of the 1950s of Hollington Red sandstone whose light-salmon-pink colour alludes directly to the building's first occupier, the Financial Times. It also distinguishes the building from its older Portland-stone neighbours, notably the nearby St Paul's Cathedral. When the bold new main entrance was added in 1992, the plinth came from the same Staffordshire quarry as the original stone and helps unite the high-tech, heavily glazed work by Hopkins Architects with the facade of the earlier building.

Figure 4.27
Stone from the same quarry connects different decades of design at Bracken House, City of London.

Slate

Used in buildings for centuries and nationwide from the eighteenth century, when transportation became easier by canal and rail, slate serves as a roofing, walling, cladding and flooring material and was even used to form damp-proof courses in walls. Today, imitation slate products are widely used for reasons of cost. These tend to have a bland uniformity of colour, shape and texture when compared with the natural Welsh slates roofing the terraces of many towns.

Metals

With a long tradition of use in buildings, metals of varying types are employed as structural elements, cladding, decorative layers, finishes and to form individual fittings. Some are hot-forged by blacksmiths. The beauty, balance and proportion of the work is a result of the skill and imagination of the maker. Others are worked on site and make an equally important contribution practically and aesthetically.

Wrought iron

Made until the mid-20th century, wrought iron is a forgeable ferrous material that has been replaced by modern mild steel. When heated and worked, wrought iron and mild steel are clearly different materials but as a finished, painted item they are hard to identify by sight, even for a blacksmith. When compared with mild steel, wrought iron generally offers a greater resistance to corrosion, plasticity when hot and tensile strength when cold.

The use of bold and often intricate ironwork in the form of gates and screens burgeoned in the 17th century. Today such work in wrought iron is rare but can be exceptional, as demonstrated by the 5m wide and 5m high reredos designed by John Maddison for Ely Cathedral's Lady Chapel in Cambridgeshire. The work has been executed using traditional techniques. Instead of modern electric welding of joints, the time-honoured use of wedges has been employed on the screen.

Cast iron

The first significant use of cast iron for architectural work was in 1714 when railings were erected around St Paul's Cathedral in London. Early examples were relatively coarse, although by the end of the Georgian

Figure 4.28
A cast-iron hopper head, aluminium downpipe, lead flashing and stainless steel fastenings work in harmony with oak (far left).

Figure 4.29
Wrought ironwork reredos in Ely Cathedral (left).

period production techniques had improved considerably. A greater countrywide use of cast iron occurred after the 1851 Great Exhibition and was often manufactured locally. Cast-iron rainwater goods are still frequently specified for listed buildings due to their texture and overall aesthetic but the biggest challenge is maintenance since, without regular painting, they rust. Cast-aluminium rainwater goods are often used in place of cast iron as they offer a similar appearance without the upkeep.

Steel

Steel had largely supplanted wrought and cast iron by the 1890s because of its strength and workability and today has many applications within construction. Stainless steel has a particular role, adding a feeling of quality to schemes designed within the historic context and is ideal for both new and repair work. Its durability as a structural component is particularly valued as it is non-rusting and does not react with or stain timber.

The ability to use steel in high-quality design is clearly illustrated at Ely Cathedral, where the lettering within the new altar in the Lady Chapel was water cut through half-inch steel sheet and then gilded. Rather than mechanically texturing the surface, the steel was left outside to rust and pit so has a roughness that gives it life and depth.

Weathering steel

Weathering or Cor-Ten steel is a material that eliminates the need for painting as it takes on a natural stable oxidised layer and a rust-like appearance. Particularly effective when used in conjunction with traditional materials, it was chosen by Haworth Tompkins for the construction of the Dovecote Studio.

The patina of the new structure complements the brick of what remained of the existing building but, more importantly, it feels at home on the Suffolk coast where rusty steel is often seen in the marine environment. The material was used to equal effect by Chris Dyson Architects at the Gasworks, Gloucestershire, and referenced both the original cottage's lean-to porch of rusty steel and the industrial heritage of the site.

Lead

Employed for roofing and flashings and, in the past, for rainwater goods, lead is a traditional material that can have a notable aesthetic and practical role in new buildings. The distinctive grained texture of old lead

Figure 4.30
Modern cast-aluminium rainwater goods (right).

Figure 4.31
Water-cut lettering forms part of the altar design in Ely Cathedral's Lady Chapel (far right).

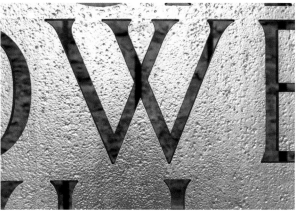

sheet is due to it being cast on beds of sand. The grainy texture tends to be hidden on roof sheeting/cladding as the smooth side sheds water better. With downpipes, the smooth side is the internal face and the rougher one external. Smoother, milled lead sheet was produced by a rolling process from the mid 1700s and is now the most commonly employed form of lead used in buildings. Machine-cast or direct-method lead sheet was introduced into the UK in the 1980s but, like sand-cast lead, cannot be produced to the consistent tolerances achieved by milled lead.

Lead's versatility as a building material was exploited in Bath by Donald Insall Associates to form an elliptical roof over part of the Cross Bath in 2006. This spa for bathing was erected on the site of a medieval bath and the present walls date from 1798. The new roof was added to create an entrance vestibule and cantilevered canopy with a glass apron, blending modern and traditional techniques.

Copper

With some of the same qualities and sometimes seen as an alternative to lead, copper has the advantage of being lighter and is slightly less prone to expansion and contraction. Copper was the obvious cladding choice for the Copper Kingdom Centre, and Donald Insall Associates took a sophisticated approach to how it was manipulated and detailed in order to exploit the weathering properties of the material.

The ethos of the design was to allow the materials to age well and naturally. No patination oil or pre-patination colour was applied to the copper's surface. Instead it was allowed to naturally change colour, in fact turning a dark reddish-brown within only a few weeks due to the marine environment.

Copper with a very different look was used alongside a range of materials, including render and

Figure 4.33
The Copper Kingdom
Centre's copper cladding
(right).

Figure 4.34
Internal copper alloy
cladding at All Souls
Bolton (far right).

sandstone, by OMI architects as a cladding for one of the pods within All Souls Bolton. Giving a sense of illumination and enhancing the quality of light in one area of the building's interior, the gold-coloured copper alloy shingles add a luminous quality to what is still a consecrated church.

Bronze

Widely used in architectural detailing, bronze lends itself to schemes where new and old come together. In undertaking the extension to Southwark Cathedral in London in 2000, Richard Griffiths Architects employed the material extensively in fittings because its dark, lustrous qualities blend well with the new architecture and setting. For its work at Bracken House, Hopkins Architects exploited the material to an

even greater extent, with tripartite bronze castings resting on the stone piers, supporting the gunmetal structural bays. This follows the precedent set for the use of bronze for the windows of the 1950s buildings and works in harmony with the Hollington Red sandstone.

Pollard Thomas Edwards selected bronze rain-screen cladding for the Granary in Barking as it offers a modern aesthetic and detailing to contrast with the historic context but also because it is a traditional building material. Durability was another consideration, as was the way it would weather on the building's different aspects.

The detailing it provides is crisp and clean while the subtle undulations of the panels

Figure 4.35
Clerkenwell Cooperage,
with patinated bronze
cladding.

lighten and soften the aesthetic of the extension. For its Clerkenwell Cooperage scheme in London, Chris Dyson Architects employed a system of patinated bronze cladding panels and glass to distinguish the bedroom addition from the early 1900s brick structure. The bronze panels give a monolithic quality to the vertical extension that rises from the top of the former brewery, while the patination increases the richness of the colour.

Glass

The invention of float glass in 1959 revolutionised glass-making, resulting in lower production costs and a higher-quality product. What was sacrificed was the material's traditional beauty: old glass has natural imperfections due to the manufacturing process that distort reflections and cause it to come alive in the sun.

Figure 4.36
Natural irregularities in old glass give character to the facades of many old buildings.

When employing glass, consideration must be given to issues beyond the lines that appear on a drawing. Light emissions through the material at night may cause nuisance, potentially distracting from the historic and rural environment. Inside the building, glare and overheating may be issues. Rarely does glass appear fully transparent from all angles, yet it is often imagined as such at the planning stage; reflections can be intrusive and may cause problems for an external observer or the occupant.

One of the challenges of using glass is how it ages over time. The inbuilt beauty of old glass has allowed it to remain attractive in the majority of circumstances where it survives. New glass poses more of a problem. Invariably it is visualised as a crisp, clean design component so, for it to work in context, it must retain its good looks. This is not always the case – pollution, algal growth and scratching can all degrade its appearance if a rigorous maintenance regime is not in place. Modern glass can be superlative. The material's

Figure 4.37
Reflective glazing helps the Hunsett Mill extension, Norfolk, merge into its environment (far left).

Figure 4.38
Glass is an essential element at the Holburne Museum, Bath (left).

ability to reflect trees and sky has been fully exploited at Hunsett Mill, helping the building merge into the landscape.

The extension to the Holburne Museum is similarly striking. It is constructed using glass and faience and the appearance of these surfaces responds to the clouds, the sun and the rain while contrasting with the Bath stone of the original Grade I listed building. The use of low-iron glass ensures both high levels of light transmission and the transparency of the building envelope, allowing natural light to enter and interact with the spaces and objects within the extra 800 sq m of gallery space created.

Coloured glass

Stained and coloured glass has been used in buildings since the Middle Ages. An example of twentieth century use can be seen in the abstract design by John Piper of the 195 panes of the Baptistry Window of Coventry Cathedral, which range from white to deep colours. More recently, the Millennium window created by Benjamin Finn for Southwark Cathedral's Garry Weston Library alludes to the area's history, including highly detailed designs that show views of the River Thames, as well as sacred references.

Figure 4.39
Stained glass in the Millennium Window, in the Garry Weston Library, Southwark Cathedral, London.

Concrete

Figure 4.40
Precast concrete 'Gothic' ribs in the Garry Weston Library, Southwark Cathedral, London.

Modern concrete contradicts much of what is celebrated about traditional materials, such as natural patination, but it increasingly has a place in the architecture of the historic environment. Indeed, as the National Theatre, opened in 1976, demonstrates, it is a material that needs to be considered carefully in matters of conservation or extension.

Along with weathering steel, concrete was employed in the new work at Snape Maltings. Rather than creating a smooth and minimalist look, Haworth Tompkins took its cue from other concrete structures in the surrounding marsh landscape, including the weatherbeaten Second World War pillboxes where the aggregate is exposed, the surface scoured away by the salt wind.

Within the extension to Southwark Cathedral, Richard Griffiths Architects looked for a material that could provide the ribs of a Gothic structure without it being masonry, and opted for concrete. The structure of the upper part of the building is formed of precast concrete ribs and beams that incorporate a Portland stone aggregate and are clearly new .

Composites

A variety of new materials is available to the designer and combining these with modern design in a historic setting offers enormous opportunities. One example is the jigsaw of Corian panels employed by Alison Brooks Architects to clad the Lens House extension to an 1860 north London home in 2012. Corian is a lightweight, dimensionally stable, completely solid, non-porous and homogenous material. Its smooth finish means that the faceted sides of the Lens House reflect light in varying shades from silver-white to black, depending on the weather.

Figure 4.41
Corian panels employed at
the Lens House, London.

Figure 4.42
Clay plasters used in the
conversion of an old
building into a loft
apartment.

FINISHES

The choice of finishes is an important design consideration for the appearance of a building. Finishes that are natural, traditional and low impact environmentally work well alongside older structures due to their mellow appearance and their ability to take on the patina of age.

Limewash is the most traditional and natural of all finishes and may be used to great effect in new work providing the substrate has a degree of suction (capilliarity); it is not durable on non absorbant surfaces such as cement renders, masonry paints and hard bricks.

Lead paints were commonly used for joinery items in the past but are now banned except for use on certain categories of listed and scheduled buildings. Linseed oil paints offer a good alternative for internal and external joinery, both old and new. As it dries, linseed oil paint forms a flexible film so is more resilient to cracking than many other coatings. Over time the surface of the paint oxidises, becoming matt, but the wood remains protected and the look is attractive.

Clay paints are another natural product suitable for interiors and they provide a soft matt finish, good coverage, breathability and durability. Some clay paints are self-coloured by their natural mineral content. The large amount of clay in the paint means that it absorbs moisture, helping to regulate the internal humidity of a building.

Clay plasters are breathable and have long been used for interior walls and ceilings. They help to regulate temperature and humidity, so are ideal for areas such as kitchens and bathrooms, while also acting as an acoustic absorber. Today they are available ready mixed and provide through body colour in a range of shades that can be finished to create a wide variety of textures and patterns.

Roughcast, known as 'harling' in Scotland and northern England, describes a lime render finish mixed with pea gravel thrown onto the face of a building. Visually interesting due to its textural quality, its increased surface area serves to maximise evaporation and protect against driving rain. Insulating lime plasters and renders are increasingly used to improve the thermal performance of walls while allowing their appearance and breathability to be retained.

BUILDABILITY

Material choices are often driven by practical constraints relating to the environment in which the new work is being undertaken. This was the case at All Souls Bolton, where it was necessary to bring everything associated with the new internal structures in through the west door. With the size of individual components governed by the size of the door, a composite system was chosen to build the pods that comprised a steel frame and structural insulated panel system (SIPs). This provides the structural strength and thermal performance required to create what is effectively a building within a building. The build-up used over this structure is not the same throughout. A number of different types of plasterboard – depending on whether they had to fulfil additional fire, sound or insulation requirements – and various render finishes were employed.

Weight savings

The engineering challenges involved in adding to old buildings can be immense and in some cases lightweight materials may be appropriate when introducing new elements as they reduce the weight placed on the existing structure. At Chedworth Roman Villa, Feilden Clegg Bradley Studios developed a timber-framed solution which bears straight onto the Roman walls. This conservation shelter protects the most significant archaeological remains while avoiding any suggestion of reconstruction of the Roman villa. The new building clearly recognises the juxtaposition of old and new. All elements of the timber cladding are of untreated European larch, grown on the National Trust's estate in its managed forest at Ashridge in Hertfordshire.

MATERIAL AGEING

One of the many joys of old buildings and the traditional materials used in their construction is the way they age and patinate over time. This is of course an accidental attribute as few craftspeople or builders are likely to have thought about how a structure would age, even in the comparatively short term, let alone after centuries.

'It's about understanding the ways that building materials and details weather and move and what that does to the aesthetic of design. If the true intent is for a building to last fully intact for more than 60 years, it should be designed to look as good, if not better, in 60 years than it does when it's built. Designers should recognise that we have the intelligence about materials, detailing and craftsmanship to be able to achieve that.'

Geoff Rich, Feilden Clegg Bradley Studios

Surface finishes that are seen and accepted today are often different to those of the original, having changed not only through the inevitable process of ageing but through fashion, neglect and technical interventions. The fine lines of joinery will have been obscured by a build-up of paint layers, the painted interior surfaces of churches may have been lost or whitewashed over, or original render has been removed from rubble masonry walls leaving an appearance very different from that intended.

The relative ageing process of different materials should be an important consideration when specifying them, especially in the context of the historic environment. Both longevity and appearance are factors. Materials such as stone and timber, which can be used and enjoyed for their lively surface, character and colour, tend to weather satisfactorily, enduring well and looking better as they age. In the case of Portland stone, some feel the architectural effect is enhanced by the 'shadow' provided by pollution deposits and believe that architects in the past anticipated this effect.

A fact to note is that some materials, like timber, have to be considered carefully in respect of weathering on different faces of a building. For example, the way timber cladding is affected by the weather can be markedly different on north and south elevations.

Many materials, such as copper and lead, accumulate an attractive natural patina. Indeed the distinctive green that some copper can take on is often a design intent. The appearance of timber can change significantly, with some, such as oak, assuming an attractive silvery grey colour.

Figure 4.44
Oak weathers gracefully over time.

'As they last so long, buildings need to have a positive response to their environment, they need to be above all beautiful and allow things to change and to fit well. It is very much about each project but, where possible, using natural materials is a much easier way of dealing with ageing in the context of historical buildings because they do weather well.'

Chris Dyson, Chris Dyson Architects

CHAPTER 5:
FORMS OF ADAPTATION

Adapting old buildings constructs a future on the past. Every intervention sets down another layer of history and, whether it sits politely or is something bold, each action presents a challenge and should demonstrate the transformational power of well-understood design.

Not all buildings are equal. Some are easily changed and the work is minimal or uncontroversial; others are less straightforward, or are seen as art due to their provenance or quality. In reality, many old buildings fall into neither of these extremes, but they are loaded with their own historical narrative and deserve thoughtful work that will ensure their future.

Styles today are diverse and for a design to succeed the emphasis must be on a carefully considered and well-executed response. Creating good architecture in the historic environment is not restricted to traditional details or materials; it relies on finding a solution through form, geometry, texture and colour, and then stitching these elements into the historic fabric. It requires approaching an old building with care, affection and understanding – on the one hand making a connection with the architects and builders of yesterday, respecting their choices and craft, while on the other, creating an environment that responds to immediate needs and enables the building to continue its long life.

Buildings change from the moment they are completed, even if only subtly. In his book *How Buildings Learn*, Stewart Brand references Frank Duffy, co-founder of the British design firm DEGW, who defined a building as having four layers: Shell, Services, Scenery and Set. Brand takes this further, expanding the layers to six: Site, Structure, Skin (exterior surfaces), Services, Space plan (interior layout) and Stuff (furniture and possessions).

Figure 5.00
Thermae Bath Spa, where new work has regenerated the site of the ancient hot spring (left).

Figure 5.01
The Mill, Scottish Borders, now a home but with the character of the original building retained (right).

Two things become obvious. Firstly, the changes to these layers occur at different speeds. Secondly, change does not happen only through conscious, design-based decisions; it comes about as a result of everyday use and is often one of the reasons we like old buildings: organic accretion, the ageing of materials and the marks of history, which are all adaptive and positive processes.

REPAIRING, UPDATING, ADDING

The adaptation of old buildings is a complex process but the way it is tackled is the same as with any building type. Successful outcomes may be realised through a number of levels of change that require different skills, strategies and types of intervention which may be undertaken on their own or as a whole. An approach that pulls together the disparate needs of the building and its occupants through each level of change will be the most successful.

Figure 5.02
Pointing with lime mortar, a key repair material for old buildings.

At the simplest and least destructive level, a building is given new life through careful and skilful repair using appropriate materials and craftsmanship. This may involve only minor repairs and a coat of paint. In some cases the building might need to be made windproof and watertight through works to the roof, walls and other elements of the external envelope. In the worse cases, significant stabilisation of the structure will be called for.

The updating of a building is likely to build upon the philosophy of skilful repair but inevitably involves more fundamental change and is likely to have a direct impact on the building's fabric. At their simplest, renovation projects call for updated services and some rearrangement of internal spaces; at the more extreme they can result in significant remodelling and structural interventions. Following on from the processes of repair, renovation and updating might come the third level of change, an addition in the form of an extension, insertion or the weaving in of new elements.

All of these approaches were followed at Cardigan Castle in Wales. Purcell was commissioned to undertake an initial condition survey and an appraisal to determine a future use for the castle, which is a Scheduled Ancient Monument with six separately listed Grade II* buildings within its curtilage. Initial work included repairing the castle's curtain walls. Subsequently the buildings within the walls were repaired, conserved and upgraded with new holiday accommodation, small-business workspace, conference facilities and a restaurant added, the latter cantilevering out above the old walls.

ARCHITECTURAL SOLUTIONS

While lessons can be learnt from the past, design is also a continuous process of experimentation and discovery. It is needlessly limiting to focus on one solution, building type or architectural discipline and false to assume that a solution that has worked in one place can be automatically applied to a different building. From a positive perspective, there is a huge body of knowledge and techniques that can be shared between commercial, residential and religious projects, and an opportunity to embrace new materials alongside the traditional, without being bound by convention or dogma.

Insertions

Elegantly designed elements inserted within original structures prove time and again to be the solution for old buildings that need a fresh start, particularly those that have decayed or fallen into a ruinous state. Both Astley Castle and Blencowe Hall were given new life in this way.

Assimilating the new into the old is crucial to the success of such schemes and vital if the integrity of both the buildings and the setting is to be retained. Meeting constantly changing needs over five centuries, Magdalen College, Oxford, has been extended and adapted on various occasions in ways that have been of their time and sensitive to the context of the site. The college's Grade II* listed Longwall Library and quadrangle were designed by Giles Gilbert Scott in the 1930s and are an adaptation of Magdalen College School, originally designed by JC Buckler in the mid-nineteenth century.

Within the restricted site of this historic setting, Wright & Wright Architects developed a library to meet today's needs by reworking the interior, landscaping the quadrangle and carefully integrating a new L-shaped extension. The work was completed in 2016. The old and new read as one entity and incorporate the functions of a modern building while increasing the space to accommodate 120 readers instead of the previous 12 readers and a librarian.

Different from the collegiate setting, but no less demanding, is the insertion of retail space within old buildings, especially when the storefront faces a historic market square designed by seventeenth century architect Inigo Jones. In 2010 this was the challenge facing San Francisco-based practice Bohlin Cywinski Jackson with the Apple Store in London's Covent Garden, which occupies a Grade II listed nineteenth century former hotel and adjacent warehouse building.

Figure 5.03
Section through Magdalen College's Longwall library, Oxford.

The design process was guided by a respect for the building's original fabric, which was seen as a site-specific backdrop for the Apple products displayed. Original ironwork and brick contrast with the newly inserted glass elements – including staircases – that provide a fresh and unifying quality. Thanks to a skylight framed in stainless steel, the former delivery forecourt for horse-drawn traffic now serves as a large central atrium. Externally, the entry portico allows the glazing of the storefront to step back from the public square and market hall, providing the facade with depth and intrigue rather than it being overpowered by the retail experience within.

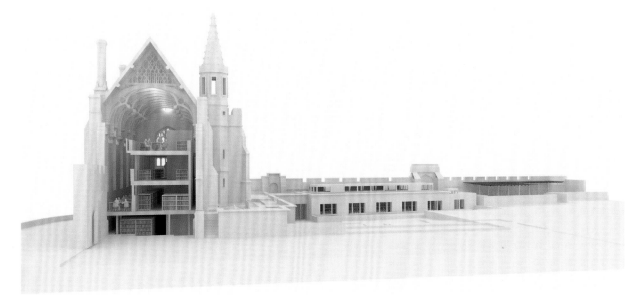

In Bath, Haworth Tompkins responded to a brief drawn up by a group of 9 to 18 year-olds when designing The Egg Theatre. This children's theatre, with its flexible seating plan, was inserted within the crumbling Bath-stone skin of a Grade II listed Victorian building, alongside the Theatre Royal.

In the past, the building's interior had undergone substantial change, which had destroyed much of the original fabric. The challenge of creating a theatre with a rehearsal area above and a café and foyer below was considerable and needed an innovative structural solution to avoid undermining the historic foundations. This resulted in the egg-shaped auditorium which has given the theatre its name.

Throughout the building, old and new coexist with striking effect. In corridors, on staircases and within the acting area itself, the original stone walls frequently emerge to contrast with the upholstery and playful translucent red corrugated plastic of the auditorium walls. Unusually for a theatre, there are floor-to-ceiling windows at the back of the stage that introduce natural light but which can be blocked out with shutters during performances.

An insertion of a very different kind was made into the shell of a former grain threshing mill in the Scottish Borders. Abandoned 70 years ago, the mill was part of a collection of disused farm buildings cut into a hill and overlooking a valley. The client's brief to WT Architecture for The Mill called for a modern holiday retreat that retained the character of the original building but was comfortable and well-insulated. The walls of the ruin were consolidated with lime mortar and an independent timber-framed structure, clad in black-stained weatherboarding, was inserted within them.

The insertion rises above the old stone walls to reveal the upper portion of the dark new timber, the windows and the pitched roof, laid with traditional slates. Most of the other windows in the new structure align with openings in the old stonework, although additional openings with galvanised steel frames were added to the south gable to provide views across the valley.

Even more exacting than creating individual homes within old buildings is the challenge of turning historic structures and environments into successful housing schemes. Architect Woodfield Brady worked with Thomas Homes to create the Old Railway Quarter, a mixed-use development at the heart of a conservation

Figure 5.05
Foyer of the Egg Theatre,
Bath, within a Victorian
shell.

area in Swindon, Wiltshire. At its core are buildings rooted in the history of the Great Western Railway, including a Grade II* listed chain-testing house, which will become a mini-museum, as well as two major 1840s workshops with cast-iron trussed roofs where springs were manufactured.

Accommodation, in the form of 56 mezzanine and loft apartments, has been carefully slotted into the vast interiors of the old spring shops, leaving the edges of the buildings relatively untouched. The homes are accessed via shared 'streets' running within the old buildings that maintain a sense of the original volume and industrial past. This is helped by the presence of the original steel trusses, the retention of the massive stone walls and the use of appropriate new materials that provide a tactile and honest feel.

Throughout the scheme original access points and features were retained wherever possible. A former smithy yard was revealed by removing a later roof structure and is presented as a secluded shared courtyard, integrated between the linear forms of the original buildings.

Weavings

Figure 5.06
The Mill: modern holiday
accommodation within a
ruin, Scottish Borders.

While insertions are possible in cases where there is a clearly defined space, many buildings do not offer the same freedom so new work has to be worked into and around the existing fabric.

Faced with the threat of invasion by Napoleon in the early nineteenth century, the British government built a chain of Martello towers. Martello Tower Y is one of these small defensive forts dating from 1808 and stands on the Suffolk coast at Bawdsey, in an Area of Outstanding Beauty. In the purest sense it is a clear story of integrating new with old.

With its status as a Scheduled Ancient Monument, it took a committed multidisciplinary team to ensure that the design vision remained intact throughout the two years of complex planning negotiations required to turn the derelict building into a home. The tower is constructed of some 750,000 bricks and the team was determined that the masonry should be the star, with the new work woven into the original fabric as lightly as possible.

Figure 5.07
Old Railway Quarter, Swindon, with the apartments' front doors on the right.

The scheme's success results largely from the design of the undulating new roof. Historically the roof was a flat gun platform with a cloverleaf layout that allowed the large cannons on top to operate through a full 360 degrees. Careful consideration was therefore essential before adding any form of structure which might be visible externally, especially from the coastal walk.

In creating the concept for the roof extension, Piercy&Company took inspiration from the geometry of the existing building and the sculptural interior of vaulted brickwork. Formed with an ellipse shape, the extension occupies one side of the roof. The new structure, completed in 2010, is lifted and has a curved skirt of frameless glass that achieves the illusion of the roof floating. In practical terms, this window provides panoramic views of the sea from the combined kitchen, living and dining area within; a terrace offers outside space. Viewed externally, the elliptical roof extension is a discreet, offset element that has a harmonious relationship with both the tower and its coastal setting. The 3D lightweight curved roof structure was prefabricated off site using computer-generated cutting patterns and is constructed of steel and laminated plywood, lightly tethered by five pairs of tension bars that provide the only structural connection between the new and existing building.

The ruins of the eighteenth century, Grade B listed White House on the Isle of Coll, in the Hebrides off the northwest coast of Scotland, have provided the setting for a new house that echoes the character of the ruin. The zigzag split in the ruin, which contributes greatly to the identity of the house and is integral to the character of WT Architecture's scheme, was retained and consolidated through repointing with lime mortar and the careful insertion of concrete lintels and discreet stainless steel straps. While a portion of the ruin is occupied, almost half remains roofless and this part provides a courtyard garden, helping to preserve the appearance of the original house.

A new wing of domestic accommodation is connected by a glazed living room link, while the massing of the new structures is broken down so they are mannerly but have strength of form in their own right. Their

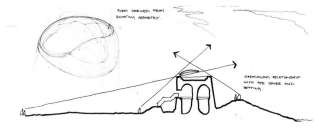

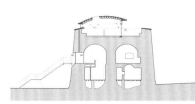

Figure 5.08
Martello Tower Y: sight lines from nearby locations (far left).

Figure 5.09
Working new elements into the massive walls of Martello Tower Y (left).

weaving into the site gains further integrity from a massive drystone wall that provides shelter and extends into the landscape, forming a link to ancient patterns of enclosure. Although directly contrasting with the vernacular, further connection with the landscape and sea views is made through the expansive glazing of the new building.

An even more intricate weaving of the old and new was undertaken in Bath when Grimshaw and Donald Insall Associates worked together to create the Thermae Bath Spa complex through a process of both new design and conservation. The scheme, regenerated an area of the city which had become uninviting and unvisited and involved one new building and five historic buildings, including the Grade I listed Cross Bath and the Grade II* listed Hot Bath.

Within the Cross Bath the remnants of the Georgian pump room were reinterpreted with the introduction of an oval pool and a cantilevered canopy, together with glazed changing rooms and entrance vestibule. Grimshaw's new centrepiece is the state-of-the-art New Royal Bath, inserted on the site of the only unlisted building. This is a striking interplay between circles, curves and the rectilinear lines of the cube that forms the main volume, while the material palette of golden Bath stone, concrete, stainless steel and high-performance glazing creates a bridge between old and new. Internally, the design knits the buildings together; physical differences in floor levels are resolved through the use of split levels and transparent bridges that open up vistas through the space.

A vastly different set of challenges faced Wilkinson Eyre in creating a scheme to transform Giles Gilbert Scott's 1940s Grade II listed New Bodleian Library in Oxford from what was essentially a book storage facility into a public building, which opened in 2015, now known as the Weston Library.

'Understanding the geometry of an existing building is really important. Although it doesn't apply to every project, with the Martello Tower the existing form "told" us how to design the new work. The cam-shaped radial plan of the existing building sets up a series of curves. This geometry was used to create the gentle double curves of the new extension so there is a strong relationship of old and new.'

Stuart Piercy, Piercy&Company

Figure 5.10
A ruinous sense is maintained at the White House, on the Isle of Coll (right).

Figure 5.11
The Cross Bath, in Bath, modernised, functioning and accessible (far right).

Internally, a large new public space was created. Externally, the practice implemented a scheme that moved the main entrance to give direct access to this space. This required the opening up of a rather forbidding facade into something much lighter and more welcoming in a highly sensitive location immediately opposite Nicholas Hawksmoor's Clarendon Building and Christopher Wren's Sheldonian Theatre. To achieve this, the plinth was removed and the building's original pilasters were converted into columns, thus creating an arcade with a glazed facade pushed back from the front of the building. This is in shadow when viewed from the street and provides depth and interest that was lacking in Gilbert Scott's original.

Figure 5.12
The arcade created at the Weston Library, Oxford.

Juxtapositions

Used in the historic environment, well-executed juxtaposition allows the old to remain clearly readable against the new, with visual separation created by distinct material and design differences. Despite these clearly set boundaries, there is inherent integration and sympathy: the two structures function together as a new and successful entity. Pollard Thomas Edwards successfully used the technique of juxtaposition at the Granary, on Barking Creek, Barking. The scheme saw the creation of new, self-contained and openly

Figure 5.13
The Granary – a sizeable but complementary juxtaposition of mass.

assertive design alongside the sensitive conversion of the nineteenth century building. The added structure, although distinctly modern and different, has a shape, colour and texture that is in harmony with the old.

In a very different way, Chris Dyson Architects employed juxtaposition at the Gasworks, in Gloucestershire. Cor-Ten steel was chosen for the cladding of the courtyard extension to help make clear the distinction between it and the stone-built cottage to which it is linked. While they are very different, the forms of the two buildings are sympathetic and benefit from one another's company. Such schemes demonstrate the power of appropriate shape and scale and how materials and construction details influence the success of the built form, giving life and relevance to an old building in both practical and aesthetic terms.

In the case of the Whitworth Gallery, part of the University of Manchester, MUMA (McInnes Usher McKnight Architects) opened up the uncompromising brick facade to the rear of the existing 1908 building. Elegant glass, stainless steel and brick additions were devised which see two wings extend into the park, one containing a café, the other housing a study centre and conservation rooms. The addition, although striking, defers to the aesthetics and materials of the Edwardian museum and, since opening in 2015, is a good measure of what makes a successful scheme.

Figure 5.15
The extension to the Whitworth Gallery, Manchester.

Figure 5.16
The British Museum's
World Conservation and
Exhibitions Centre,
London.

At the British Museum, London, Rogers Stirk Harbour + Partners conceived the nine-storey World Conservation and Exhibitions Centre as a new wing, made up of a cluster of pavilions. To make the transition from the classical facades of the existing museum and the domestic scale of the neighbouring properties, the height and mass of the new building were carefully considered so it is slightly lower than the neighbouring museum, with a gap delineating the junction.

The new wing is constructed using a steel frame with a rain-screen cladding of Portland stone panels and kiln-formed glass planks. In contrast to the solid nature of the stone of the older building, this 50-mm-thick stone is non-structural, a fact made clear as it stops around 500 mm from the ground.

Eric Parry's extension to Bath's Holburne Museum turns juxtaposition into an art form. Glimpsed from a distance there is an unexpected ethereal quality to the extension added to the rear of the Grade I listed building. No attempt has been made to mimic the classical detailing or solidity of the Bath-stone original, which dates from the late eighteenth century. While the glass cladding and ceramic fins of the extension are unashamedly modern in form, the use of materials and layering to the facade creates an interplay of shadows, lightness and reflectivity made all the more vibrant because of the parkland setting. Unusually, the top of this structure is more solid than the base, the inversion adding a remarkable lightness to its form.

'We tried to pick up on as many clues as we could from the old museum building next door to inform the design and then used our own devices to tell a story and very much make a modern building without apology, but one that had some sympathies and consistencies with the old.'

John McElgunn,
Rogers Stirk Harbour + Partners

Although the new building's footprint is less than half that of the original, this was a controversial and bold intervention but one that re-established the axis through the building from the city to an eighteenth century pleasure garden. In common with many such schemes, the extension to the Holburne Museum answers the need for more exhibition space with the creation of two additional floors: about 60 per cent of the exhibits now on display had not previously been on show. Disabled access, a café and room for education have also been provided.

Glass boxes

The glass box extension when added to old buildings provokes mixed reactions. As a device it seems like the perfect solution: more than any other form, it shouts contrast and a new phase of building.

But is a glass box good design in the context of the historic environment? Often reflectivity and invisibility are claimed as virtues. The answer lies in being intelligent and realistic about the role of the box alongside the building that it serves. Interventions are undertaken to resolve a problem and, to be successful, the choice of material and the language of design must be appropriate. If glass is chosen simply for visual effect it is likely to fail. More than any other form, the glass box draws attention both to itself and to the mechanisms that are required to make it work. Often it fails when it is made to do more than was intended technically, so junctions become visually clumsy and convoluted engineering solutions are required to deal with issues such as thermal efficiency. These are not insurmountable challenges, as evidenced by the fact that a glass extension to a historic structure can be breathtakingly beautiful, providing it is extremely well detailed and engineered, as with the Holburne Museum .

Figure 5.17
The Holburne Museum, Bath, with its bold juxtaposition of materials.

Echoes of form

Sometimes the best solution when working with ruins or where there are elements missing from an ensemble is the re-creation of the shapes of the former buildings, but reinterpreted through new design and different materials. By drawing close parallels with what has been lost, memories can be stimulated and kept alive and new structures may be allowed to sit more comfortably within the historic context.

This is the case at Laidneskea Steading, near Aberfeldy, Perthshire, where Simpson & Brown Architects undertook the repair and conversion of nineteenth century buildings originally built in local

Figure 5.18
Traditional forms reinstated at Laidneskea Steading, Perthshire.

stone as a model farm. The buildings, arranged around an open-ended courtyard, had become redundant and were falling into dereliction. Evidence existed of a circular horse-gang and a walled lean-to wing. These elements were reinstated in 2007 to form four houses arranged around the courtyard. New openings were kept to a minimum and traditional detailing was employed on the existing buildings while the new additions were approached in a more contemporary way with extensions added in timber to create clear articulation between old and new. The construction of a new house on the footprint of an earlier building added to the overall group.

Few new buildings echo the form of their host more closely than the Dovecote Studio in Suffolk. The Cor-Ten steel module matches the form of the original nineteenth century building and was constructed outside as a single unit before being carefully craned into the space between what remained of the original brick walls. Repairs to the brickwork of the existing structure were kept to a minimum and were limited to stabilisation prior to the steel unit being inserted. The decaying joinery of the windows was left untouched and vegetation growing over the ruin has been allowed to contribute to the natural process of ageing and decay.

Designed by Reiach and Hall Architects to echo the simple pitched roof of the traditional waterfront warehouses, a new building at the Pier Arts Centre in Stromness, Orkney, stands on one of the piers that characterise the historic town. Inside is a temporary gallery space along with service areas and, in the attic, the collection archive of acclaimed contemporary art. The building is clad in black – rather than the dominant stone of the vernacular – but the facade shifts from solid to void, black zinc ribs alternating with translucent glass infills. The spacing of the ribs echoes the original gallery's rafters. Gable-on, the new building appears solid but dissolves as the viewer moves, allowing the original pier building to gain prominence.

Another quayside scheme is the Copper Kingdom Centre. Historically copper ore was delivered to the bins that form the basis of the new building via tramlines before being shipped around the coast of Britain, or overseas. Donald Insall Associates created the striking modern building within the shell of the old bins by extending the original structure with simple lime-mortared stonework, a slate roof and through the addition

Figure 5.19
The Pier Arts Centre, Stromness, Orkney, a traditional quayside form in new materials.

Figure 5.20
Initial concept sketch of
the Copper Kingdom
Centre, with rock face and
new chutes.

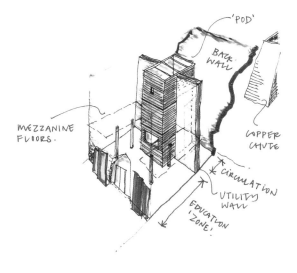

of copper cladding and industrial-scale copper and oak doors.

The project was conceived as a way of giving the structures new life and explaining Anglesey's rich history of mining and industrial heritage. Exhibition and interpretive spaces, auditorium facilities, meeting rooms and a shop are accommodated. The windows and doors have been detailed so they are hung on wheels or on telescopic hinges. By sliding back the large shutters on the outside of the building, the auditorium changes from being a dark environment to a light-filled space where artists display their works.

HOUSES

The whole gamut of architectural solutions, from insertions to echoes of form, is employed in the adaptation of houses, depending on the needs of clients and the possibilities offered by the individual buildings and their sites. The desire and requirement for change is unsurprising: 75 per cent of the UK housing stock is more than 25 years old and 20 per cent is more than 100 years old.

Some houses are already a jumble of additions made over many years and can easily accommodate further work; even Victorian and Georgian houses offer more flexibility than their original rigid social context might suggest. Others do not offer the 'loose fit' that eases the process of adaptation and, if not properly understood, certain interpretations may look ill-proportioned or appear contextually wrong. For example, historically, conservatories date from Victorian times and were only found attached to large houses so, when introduced as a new addition, they can seem out of proportion and out of place, especially where the detailing is an amalgam of invented styles.

Many of the most important attributes of successful adaptation are demonstrated by Dow Jones Architects' renovation and reconfiguration of 25 Tanners Hill, a timber-framed house in Deptford, east London, to create an art gallery and home. Maximising the use of available space by creating good circulation and introducing natural light, the scheme demonstrates how sensitivity to historic fabric and thoughtful new design can work in harmony. Old and new are woven together but are distinctly different, making the scheme fluid, readable and fresh.

The Grade II listed building is part of a terrace of small two- and three-floor houses dating from the early seventeenth century and is based on the standard London housing design for the 'lower orders' of the time, although No 25 had been rebuilt or recast around 1750. More recently it had reached a state of dilapidation.

To understand the building better, the layers were carefully peeled back. The most obvious sign of this process in the completed project is the beamed, flakily multicoloured wall that rises from the polished concrete floor of the reception and gallery space. This is both a link with the building's past and an feature in its own right and shows an empathy with the historic structure.

Dow Jones Architects' design has resulted in layered spaces with a central open courtyard that acts as a

light well at the heart of the scheme. To one side a skewed corridor adds perspective, connecting the gallery reception area with the top-lit kitchen to the rear in what was once a small and separate Victorian stable building.

Detailing throughout is minimal and enhanced by the elements that show through, charting the building's history. Nowhere is this more evident than in the kitchen, where the stark modern plaster and polished concrete floor contrasts with an almost archaeological layering of stone coping, clay tiles, soot-crusted bricks, steelwork and rough, paint-scarred render.

Lambeth Marsh House – within the Roupell Street Conservation area in central London – is a modest two-storey terraced house built in brick for artisan workers. Dating from the 1820s, the building's run-down fabric needed repair and a sensitive approach. The work undertaken by Fraher Architects, seeks to

Figure 5.24
A former gatehouse in
Richmond Park, London,
showing an appropriate
hierarchy of scale.

understand the history of the house, while the addition of a ground-floor rear and side extension complements the building's historic features and opens up the living space with a glazed area feeding light into the building.

An extension to a former mid-nineteenth century gatehouse to London's Richmond Park demonstrates an approach on a larger scale that has resulted in the creation of a six-bedroom family home. The architectural languages of the 21st century and the Victorian era relate to each other and form a respectful dialogue within a conservation area.

McGarry-Moon Architects designed the two-storey extension using a muted palette with crafted iroko timber glulam meeting sharp board-marked concrete walls. This restrained but striking palette is comfortable next to the clay tile hanging and brick of the cottage, while the meeting between the two is lightened with glass and timber.

A somewhat bolder and more uncompromisingly modern extension was added to Wakelins, a Grade II listed Tudor farmhouse in Suffolk. The oak-clad, two-storey structure connects to the existing house at ground and first-floor levels and provides a library and study on the ground floor, with master bedroom and bathroom upstairs.

Vertical oak cladding has been used in a more modest way by Mole Architects in an addition to Ramblers, a small stone cottage in Pulborough, West Sussex. The extension created a utility room, bathroom and artist's studio. A frameless glass slot provides visual separation from the listed building, while further openings are formed from frameless glazing and insulated shutters that provide privacy and shading while giving added life and depth to the facade.

Figure 5.25
The timber extension at Wakelins, Suffolk, shows distinct new work (right).

Figure 5.26
Continuity of form in different materials at Ramblers (far right).

Rather than employ a contrasting material, Barker Shorten Architects married a timber-clad extension with a seventeenth century weatherboarded former village bakery in Hooe, East Sussex. Juxtaposition is achieved through the sharp lines, geometric form and unfinished timber of the new work beside the roughhewn textures and painted timber of the old building.

Figure 5.27
Hooe House, East Sussex, embraces traditional shape but is clearly new work.

One firm that has brought a sculptural approach to shape and proportion when extending old houses is Alison Brooks Architects. The Lens House saw the conversion of a derelict Victorian house in a north London conservation area into a home and workspace through the addition of a bold extension.

This wraps around the old brick walls to the side and rear of the house and is designed as a series of apertures framed and connected by large trapezoidal planes. Both roof and wall planes are of one material, either fully glazed or fully solid – there are no punched windows. To the rear, the scheme provides an up-to-date variant of a traditional bay window. The overall approach is like the folded surfaces of origami and creates an architecture without mass and weight. On the garden side, the building rests lightly on the ground with undercut walls to avoid the roots of a large walnut tree.

Figure 5.28
Forms and materials add new character at Lens House, London.

Extensions need not be large or imposing to be effective, as is demonstrated by the Flinthouse at Tidcombe Manor by Adam Richards Architects. The structure houses a front door and a kitchen and is the entrance to the self-contained wing of a Grade II* listed eighteenth century Wiltshire manor house.

Conceived as a 'primitive hut', the new building was designed to reinforce the role of the wing as a separate dwelling. The junction between the two is

Figure 5.29
The Flinthouse at Tidcombe Manor, Wiltshire, playing with scale and form.

Figure 5.30
Old Wardour House
extension, Wiltshire,
designed for light.

delineated by a wide shadow gap formed with a lead cladding. The construction is a structural cedar frame that sits within a steel gabion garden wall filled with flint gathered from the surrounding downs. Seen from a distance, the building seems tiny but the scale is deceptive and its playful character is the result of a 3m high front door and an uninterrupted roof volume achieved by using an innovative system of concealed nylon rods. Incoming light is modulated through the use of timber slats on the north and east elevations, while the west elevation is glazed up to the ridge, allowing the building to become 'a vessel for gathering evening sunlight'.

Another scheme in Wiltshire where light was a factor is Old Wardour House. The building stands beside Old Wardour Castle in Tisbury and dates from the fourteenth century, with a series of alterations made between the 1690s and the 1960s that left distinctive and eclectic traces. In the most recent extension to the house, Eric Parry Architects has taken a minimalist, non-intrusive approach with the overall aim of allowing more light into the house because it suffers shading during the winter months. Large glazed areas introduce light into the kitchen and the bedroom above, while ensuring good views out.

BARNS

Often in unspoilt rural locations, barns offer character and a direct link to the past coupled with a large internal volume and outside space. It is these attributes that are frequently seen as making barns ripe for conversion into homes or business units but they are also the factors that can make them among the most difficult projects to undertake successfully. Achieving the balance between preserving the special qualities of the building and creating a comfortable and usable interior is tricky. Due to the lack of external openings and internal division, it is easy to end up with an interior that is dark and cavernous. Even where permitted, constructing multi-room accommodation within a barn through division and the introduction of windows can be disastrous and risks losing the sense of space and history that made the building special in the first place.

The desire to introduce windows is not only to do with providing natural light and ventilation; frequently there is a desire for large windows to take advantage of countryside views. Ways of balancing this wish with

Figure 5.31
Minimal visible insertions
maintain the agricultural
feel of Feeringbury Barn,
Essex.

the need to retain the integrity of the building include using the big barn doorway onto the threshing floor as the principal source of light and employing slit windows instead of landscape-format picture windows. Flues and vents for stoves, boilers and ventilation systems should be specified with similar care and, if acceptable, are generally best accommodated to the building's rear and should be as unobtrusive as possible, with attention paid both to size, shape and colour.

Internally, the division of a barn needs to be considered in the same way as when dealing with any building with a large space, so pods, mezzanines and other devices may be useful to create the necessary comfort and accommodation while retaining open volumes and original fabric. More practically, the structural elements of some barns may be incapable of bearing the extra loads placed upon them, so providing strength and stability without the loss of original fabric is a prime concern, and one that can require the ingenuity of an engineer with experience of such structures. From a design perspective it is worth bearing in mind that barns traditionally do not have front gardens; it is the agricultural character that is important and which is easily lost. Landscaping and the positioning of domestic items such as washing lines, bin stores and cars all need sensitivity. Hudson Architects addressed many of these diverse issues when it converted the

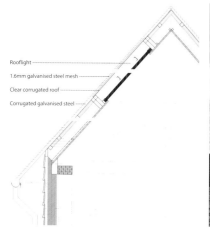

Rooflight
1.6mm galvanised steel mesh
Clear corrugated roof
Corrugated galvanised steel

Figure 5.32
Cross section of roof
elements at Feeringbury
Barn, showing concealed
rooflights (far left).

Figure 5.33
Feeringbury Barn's
unbroken roof line, where
rooflights are masked by
steel mesh (left).

Figure 5.34
Field barns are an intrinsic
feature of the Yorkshire
Dales.

Grade II listed Feeringbury Barn in Essex into a family home and artists' studios. Structural interventions were kept to a minimum and almost all the original timber framing of the sixteenth century structure was retained, with new timber used sparingly to replace timbers that were no longer usable.

The introduction of rooflights is among the biggest challenges with barn conversions and requires thought and, even where permissible, must generally be restricted to the rear roof slope if the building has a definable front and back. Feeringbury Barn would originally have been thatched but at some point had been re-roofed with corrugated sheeting. Installing any type of visible rooflight to bring daylight into the 525 sq m internal space was out of the question from a planning and conservation perspective as it would destroy the building's agricultural appearance and the aesthetic integrity of the roof.

The solution was to use large polycarbonate panels covered with a perforated steel mesh laid over the rafters. Orientated so the perforations face upwards, the rooflights are concealed from view at ground level while allowing the interior to be flooded with diffused natural light. To further echo the building's industrial nature and the texture of thatch, the mesh was chemically treated to provide a distressed, uneven look.

Not all barns lend themselves to conversion into full-time residential or business use. In the Yorkshire Dales National Park there are some 4,500 field barns, 40 per cent of which are in a poor or very poor condition. These barns are a defining component of the Dales' landscape so Feilden Clegg Bradley Studios developed an innovative design concept to conserve these historic structures while providing a sustainable use.

This is based on first repairing the barn and then inserting a free-standing 'eco-pod' to provide holiday accommodation and a source of income to the rural economy. The highly insulated timber-frame prototype was trialled in Yorkshire in 2008. It had no impact on the external appearance of the barn and is reversible if necessary.

CHURCHES AND CATHEDRALS

Despite roots that often stretch back many centuries, churches and cathedrals are facing difficult times and experiencing pressure to change. Often there is the added burden that the buildings are listed and expensive to properly maintain, particularly when they have fallen victim to the theft of materials such as lead.

Archaeology, architecture, furnishings, stained glass and historical connections, as well as the associated churchyard and setting, are all contributing factors in making churches special. The public relies on these buildings as landmarks and signs

Figure 5.35
Southwark Cathedral with
new two storey wing to
the left.

of permanence that define places and still serve as the focal point in planning decisions. Where change of use occurs, the challenges are immense. There are the questions of how to maintain the large internal volume, while making the building work in its new use, and of how to treat the redundant features such as pews, altars, rails, pulpits and wall panels, all of which may be integral to the church's history and particular identity. Some of the most interesting projects, such as the Garden Museum at St Mary-at-Lambeth and All Souls Bolton, have taken the approach of inserting more or less free-standing structures within the church, carefully working around and integrating architectural and other details.

Despite declining congregations, many churches do remain in use or are cared for as redundant churches. There are more than 16,000 Church of England buildings, often kept up by volunteers. Nevertheless, many churches are having change forced upon them by both internal and external pressures. These buildings pose hard challenges when introducing elements of new design and rarely is it possible to undertake work without, to some extent, compromising what is already there. Understanding the building's significance and why it is valued by the congregation and wider community is vital. The architect chosen must have the necessary design skills, an appropriate knowledge of architectural history and a good appreciation of church development.

The priority for the Church of England is the delivery of its mission and the desire to achieve this in a building that is flexible and comfortable. Usually the need for change is practical and involves the modest provision of facilities such as toilets, a kitchen or storage; although more ambitious plans may call for the creation of meeting rooms, offices and halls for community activities. But some works, such as underfloor heating, may be both extensive and disruptive, while promising unproven benefits. Short-term advantage may turn out to be an undesirable and destructive phase in the very long lives of these important cultural buildings.

From the beginning, careful analysis of the extent to which such facilities will be used is crucial and consideration should be given to whether new work is essential or simply desirable. Establishing the case for long-term viability is key and it must factor in upkeep and maintenance issues.

In the case of the twelfth century St Andrew's Church in Herefordshire, Communion Architects was approached by a local community organisation with a brief to transform the existing church into a multifunctional event space for five parishes which, until then, had no public meeting space. The resulting design provides a kitchen, servery and toilet, all within a wooden cube that opens out. The beauty of this solution is that the cube can be closed to restore the sacred space of the church.

There are a number of examples of the 'quiet' approach to new design in churches. Holy Trinity Church is a redundant Anglican parish church at Goodramgate, within the historic core of the medieval City of York, and is in the care of the Churches Conservation Trust (CCT). With the CCT's interest in the preservation of the special qualities of churches, the fabric is not an inconvenience to be worked around, but something that represents the history and value of the building.

To continue the successful running of Holy Trinity, the CCT recognised that

Figure 5.36
St Andrew's, Herefordshire, with carefully concealed new facilities.

Figure 5.37
Holy Trinity Goodramgate,
York: plan of extension.

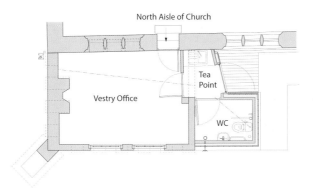

North Aisle of Church

Tea
Point

Vestry Office

WC

'We were very
conscious of the
hierarchy of what we
were doing. It may be
the latest phase, but
it's certainly not the
most important.'

Kynan Simmons, simmonsherriff

improvements were needed to the accommodation and facilities. The number of places where an addition could be made was limited, but architects simmonsherriff successfully designed a modest extension to the west side of the vestry which provides space for a toilet and a new external entrance. Design constraints existed both inside and outside as it was necessary to continue the external line of the existing vestry while providing enough width for the toilet to be wheelchair-accessible. This meant the wall thickness was restricted to 270 mm, so brick construction was impossible. Instead, the inner leaf was formed with blocks while the external finish, including the roof, is vertical oak cladding. Another reason for this choice was an awareness of the existing hierarchy of form and materials. The building dates mainly from the fifteenth century but contains elements from the twelfth to nineteenth centuries. Reflecting the various ages of construction, the church is a mixture of different building styles that make use of brick, stone, slate and clay. By being clearly different, the extension creates a further readable layer in the building's history.

A further consideration was the use of gutters and downpipes. If these had been added externally the extension would have been out of scale with the rest of the building so, instead, rainwater drains through a hidden internal gutter, allowing an uncluttered aesthetic while still being accessible for maintenance.

Figure 5.38
Holy Trinity Goodramgate:
thoughtful design in a
difficult space.

At the Church of St John the Evangelist in Leeds, the CCT was prompted to install a mezzanine floor and staircase in the base of the tower in order to improve security and use the vestry as a regional office for staff and volunteers. St John's was constructed in 1634 and is a fine and relatively scarce ecclesiastical example of seventeenth century craftsmanship at a time when few new churches were being built. Although the building is well visited, the only office space was in a separate vestry with no view into the body of the church. The insertion of the mezzanine allows those working there to have a natural vantage point through the existing high-level glazed screen between the nave and tower. This allows them to keep an eye on the activities within the church and for visitors to see that they are not alone. Architects simmonsherriff made extensive use of glass in the design of the mezzanine. Glass offered the advantages of being a thin material which could be deployed in a tight building space while having minimum visual impact. The new work is almost invisible and the building's special features, including wooden panelling and the stained glass of the west window, are not obscured. The supporting structure of the platform is anchored at four points to the tower and the mezzanine floats off it without touching the walls. For safety reasons, a clear, frameless glass balustrade rises to 1100 mm around the edges. The staircase has been designed to avoid the need for any fixings into the original fabric and, supported from the new mezzanine, rests instead on the late twentieth century quarry tiled floor.

Very different in scale is the scheme undertaken by Richard Griffiths Architects at Southwark Cathedral, London. A major, accessible entrance for the cathedral has been created and a two-storey wing added, containing a refectory on the ground floor and a function room/library on the first floor. There are also meeting rooms and a shop.

Much of the new work at Southwark is in the Arts and Crafts tradition. The language of detail in the craftsmanship and the palette of materials echo the cathedral: stone and flint, copper for the gutters and dormer windows and oak for the projecting bay windows. The ribs of the library roof and the vaults supporting the upper floors are of precast concrete. The success of the scheme stems from the level of detail and the sometimes subliminal references that link old with new; they evoke the past but the combination is undoubtedly of today.

At Norwich Cathedral the focus was on the medieval cloister at the heart of the cathedral precinct and the original refectory site next door. The work by Hopkins Architects had the goal of sustaining the future life of this ecclesiastical site while respecting its history and involved minimal alterations to the medieval fabric. Phase one of the project in 2004 saw the creation of a new refectory that replicates the scale of the original building. Kitchen, plant, toilets and other services are contained within a free-standing, single-storey timber box with a mezzanine dining area above. Over this, the roof is supported on oak columns abutting the existing library wall to one side and the repaired perimeter wall on the other. The result is a spacious and light-filled interior, helped by rooflights and triple-height spaces at either end of the

Figure 5.39
At St John the Evangelist, Leeds, glass is used for safety without blocking views.

'At Southwark Cathedral we were a bit naughty about mixing up our gothic and our classical. You must start by knowing your gothic architecture and your classical sources quite well to be able to play that game. What I try to do in my work is to say, "Okay you've got these references but they're slightly abstracted."'

Richard Griffiths, Richard Griffiths Architects

Figure 5.40
The Refectory, Norwich Cathedral, a spacious and airy re-creation.

Figure 5.41
The glass-covered internal
'street' at Southwark
Cathedral, following the
line of a Victorian alley.

Figure 5.42
The street-level entrance
pavilion for St
Martin-in-the-Fields,
London (below).

building that accommodate the entrances together with free-standing stairs and a lift.

Phase two at Norwich was the Hostry, a visitor and education centre built on the site of the original pilgrims' guest hall. This has a similar design ethos to the Refectory and embraces the same palette of mainly traditional materials, with existing walls used wherever possible.

Among the most complex church projects is the scheme by Eric Parry Architects for St Martin-in-the-Fields in London, which caters for both the local congregation and a large numbers of tourists. The site is highly significant, with a complex mix of buildings, including the Grade I listed church designed by James Gibbs in 1726, the adjacent terrace by John Nash, social care facilities, residential apartments and underground crypts and vaults. Eric Parry Architects' response connected each of the different elements of the site and included refurbishment and reconfiguration that created a vast space for meeting and rehearsal rooms, a café and a public route above ground. This involved a new underground building which includes a glazed courtyard that enables the entry of natural light as well as stairs and lift access provided by a street-level pavilion of glass and stainless steel under a shallow dome. The project brings together many forms of adaptation and, by exploiting good new design, has created a vibrant space that nurtures and sustains the community while revitalising the buildings and their setting.

CHAPTER 6:
INTERIORS

A need for more space, better circulation or extra or updated facilities is the driving force behind many interventions within old buildings. In developing a scheme, it is worth remembering that an interior is frequently rich in history and that this can help inform and drive the design process.

The interiors of old buildings are often places of intimacy and familiarity, providing continuity and security. While adding their own history, each occupant will have reacted to the still legible surroundings inherited from their predecessors. Activities historically carried out within may have links with the wider community and provide the rootedness that helps give a building its sense of place.

Equally, a building's interior may be uncomfortable and frustrating, hampering modern productivity or family life. Responding to these disparate influences when making changes or new additions is not always easy, but attempting, in an unthinking way, to remove evidence of the past is likely to prove disastrous. It is all too easy to erase those qualities and features that make a building special and interesting.

Loss of spatial integrity is incredibly damaging. For example, the extensive subdivision of a church or barn during conversion to domestic use may destroy the essence of its designed form by breaking up the large internal volumes. Proportion is everything and generous floor-to-ceiling heights contribute greatly to the feeling of wellbeing that comes from many old buildings.

Figure 6.00
New spiral staircase at Tate Britain, in London (left).

Figure 6.01
Martello Tower Y, where circulation has been improved while maintaining the connection to the past (right).

This is not to say that introducing updated and ergonomic interiors is impossible. Internal volumes are often reordered successfully and space and circulation can be dramatically improved through a well-considered scheme. Interiors do not stop with a building's intrinsic architectural components. Items such as furniture and lighting must also be considered, as well as the complexity of weaving services into a building that may once have had only the most rudimentary facilities.

More than anything, undertaking work to an old building's interior requires a clear understanding of the past and present space. Good design, skilfully executed construction and attention to detail are essential if old and new are to meet successfully and stand up to the scrutiny of close inspection.

REORDERING VOLUME

Among the most valuable aesthetic and cultural qualities of many old buildings is their internal volume. Churches and barns are built high and open, warehouses and factories are cavernous, while mansions, schools and hospitals often possess generously proportioned spaces that reflect their history and purpose.

Sometimes these spaces lend themselves to new use. This was the case when Levitt Bernstein created the Ikon Gallery from a burnt-out Victorian school building in Birmingham. Here, the volumes of the classrooms quite easily lent themselves for adaptation to flexible and airy gallery spaces that attract a wide variety of artists.

Often it is not easy to handle such space without compromise. Features that are in proportion when serving a large continuous volume become out of scale when appearing in subdivided spaces. Introducing intermediate floors may split tall windows laterally and the resulting upper-storey areas may find themselves in close proximity to massive roof timbers that consequently feel out of scale. Equally, the large volume of a church nave is unlikely to feel cosy if required to function as the sitting room of a home and will almost certainly suffer the same heating problems experienced in its previous life.

One way of viewing the interior of an old building is as a landscape into which insertions are to be made. This was how Dow Jones Architects conceptualised the design for the Garden Museum. The new work was seen as a belvedere inserted into the 'found' landscape of the medieval and Victorian church which, in the context of garden history, was entirely appropriate.

Figure 6.02
Adapted Victorian classrooms in the Ikon Gallery, Birmingham (far left).

Figure 6.03
New perspectives from the mezzanine level in the Garden Museum, London (left).

The practice developed hierarchies for how the new intervention related to the existing building, including the layering of the fabric. Most important of all was the existing stonework – ragstone rubble and Bath stone ashlar – onto which is superimposed a layer of monuments and ornament. Wood was chosen as the chief new layer in the form of cross-laminated timber (CLT). This is used both structurally and aesthetically and has a tonal resonance with the ashlar but is quieter than the primary layers of stone and ornamentation within the church.

> 'Often it's just thinking slightly differently and using very simple logic. It's that analysis of what's the best part of a building; often keeping the inside intact is very important.'
>
> Tom Bloxham, Urban Splash

Into this raw timber was inserted a further layer: the windows and doors – the only painted component. Next, a layer of graphic lettering and design was applied to the CLT to provide information, signposting and decorative elements. The final layer comprises the museum exhibits themselves.

This hierarchy helped deliver a new structure that has its own autonomy: the pale wood was like the stone but not the stone; the form of the work responds to the church but is not the church. This thinking identifies a clear conceptual idea of how the new relates to the old and how they respond specifically within the context of the building. At the same time there is a change in the sense of proportion. From the new upper level, visitors can look down into the nave for the first time and, as happens in many schemes where a mezzanine is introduced, previously unseen aspects come into view as people are brought closer to the building's roof, upper walls and monuments.

When Levitt Bernstein began considering the scheme for LSO St Luke's, in Islington, the options included dividing the space within the ruined church or introducing a mezzanine, but both would have devalued the architectural character of the interior. Equally importantly, the space for the orchestra would have become too small and acoustically poor for musicians. These factors drove the decision to leave the main volume of the old church untouched and, instead, create additional space beneath the churchyard. A large above-ground extension was out of the question because of the nature of the listed building and its setting.

Figure 6.04
Remaining pilasters and brick at LSO St Luke's, Islington, where bifurcating columns support a new roof.

The design defines an inspiring new space for music within the church by employing four massive steel columns. Independent of the original walls, these spread out like the branches of a tree to support the new roof, making it clear that the structure and galleries are an unashamedly modern intervention. No attempt has been made to disguise the raw, unplastered state of the original walls, so the building's history, with its period of ruination, is still easily appreciated. Through this mingling of old and new, the retention of the impressive uncluttered space and the introduction of retractable seating and moveable rostra, the Jerwood Hall that has been created at LSO St Luke's now satisfies many functions, from educational work and rehearsals to recitals and recordings, as well as corporate and private events.

Figure 6.05
The Matchworks,
Liverpool, with pods
housing services and
utilities.

Many interiors require a pragmatic approach. Before Urban Splash undertook its Matchworks scheme in Garston, Liverpool, which saw the conversion of a Grade II listed former match factory into offices, other developers had looked at the site and considered it too expensive to redevelop. Most saw the columns within the original 1920s building as a problem and were put off by the vast cost of removing them. Conversely, Urban Splash viewed the columns as an advantage and, instead of breaking up the space, housed kitchens, toilets and other utilities in external pods. This approach allowed for the creation of extra open-plan office space which added value to the scheme.

Equal challenges existed for Pollard Thomas Edwards when converting the eighteenth century Gunpowder Mill, in Waltham Abbey, Essex, into a headquarters for their client in 2009. Bridges, walkways and staircases inserted into the building's volume now link offices, meeting areas and workstations, at the same time allowing views through the building. The modern work is

Figure 6.06
View through Gunpowder
Mill, in Waltham Abbey,
Essex.

120

Figure 6.07
Spacious new interior of
the Weston Library,
Oxford.

expressed differently from the original through the use of two shades of colour, with a light grey for the old structure and a darker grey for the new.

Wilkinson Eyre took a different approach when creating the Weston Library. The 1940s building was originally designed as a book storage facility but, after the majority of the contents was moved to a new home, it was decided to create a scheme that capitalised on the building's heritage. Voids were introduced through the structure to frame what had been the central bookstack and bring in controlled daylight. The interventions were extensive, but the design has reinvigorated the library, creating a soaring entrance hall while improving circulation for users, making book retrieval easier and providing exhibition and seminar spaces. Further interventions include a reading room at roof level with views across the city.

Figure 6.08
Pod layout within All Souls
Bolton.

PODS

Rather as if an elegant caravan has been parked within the structure, pods provide the opportunity to create a building within a building. The pod form is highly adaptable, enabling the integration of living and working areas that minimise impact on and contact with the historic fabric, while allowing the volume of the space to be retained. An often overlooked benefit of pods is that they allow for the presence of internal environments which are heated and cooled separately from the historic structure, thereby providing stable comfort levels for occupiers without the draughts and temperature fluctuations that may exist in a building such as a church.

Pods provide all these advantages at All Souls Bolton. Respecting the building's structure was key to the success of the project as the roof has one of the widest unsupported spans of any parish church in England. Creating a series of new spaces while respecting this important feature was vital. The pods were carefully conceived and placed so as to retain an intelligible sense of the church's historic interior, with the span of the roof still clearly visible and the view of the stained glass at the east end maintained.

Very different, but just as successful, is the Pod Gallery created by Stonewood Design within the Grade II listed Home Farm Barn in South Gloucestershire. As if floating, this pod is cantilevered and forms an extension to the main house by providing a warm, dry, light and controlled environment to house a collection of watercolour paintings.

As is general with pods, this is a reversible intervention. The walls and roof of the pod stand away from the stone walls and timber roof structure of the seventeenth century barn, only touching the old building where the pod sits on the barn floor. Looking out from within the pod through its full-height glazing, the splendour of the barn is revealed, while from inside the barn the soft warm qualities of the lightweight timber structure contrast with the cold solidity of the stone.

Unlike many other pod insertions, the Pod Gallery closely mirrors the shape of the building it sits within. At the same time, it is clearly new and different but has a direct relationship with its host building. The interior feels self-contained but there is a visual connection with the outside, as the glazed windows in the gallery's walls are aligned with the external openings of the barn.

In contrast, the bathrooms and an oak spiral staircase within Feeringbury Barn in Essex have been housed in two concrete silos that were moved from another part of the building. While consciously breaking up the large space, they still allow the building's volume to be appreciated.

Two oak-clad pods introduced by Donald Insall Associates within the Copper Kingdom Centre provide both access and a reference to the original timber chutes down which copper ore was tipped into storage bins. The pods vertically penetrate the centre of each bin to form a focal point around which the natural circulation of the building unfolds. One contains a staircase, the other a staircase and a lift; both incorporate mechanical services. Internally these are painted a shade of orange taken from the colour palette found in the local copper ore. Large central rooflights, directly over the circulation stairs, provide natural light while externally giving a visual clue to the location of the original chutes.

Working with limited internal space and budget, Communion Architects used the pod form to introduce new facilities into St Andrew's Church. The build requirements were reduced to an absolute minimum, compressing all new functions into a single pod-like cube. This created meeting spaces to either side, while the cube includes an accessible toilet, houses a ground-source heat pump and, when opened out, provides a kitchen facility for food and drink preparation. It also affords storage and security for electronic and IT equipment.

SPACE AND CIRCULATION

Among the primary reasons for the extension or alteration of old buildings is the need to create extra space. Often overlooked is exactly how the existing space will be integrated with the new so that it is used effectively in the future. This is a particularly common problem with single-storey rear extensions to homes, where the design effort is focused on the extension without considering what will happen to the original rooms. Frequently these become dark, poorly ventilated 'corridors' that simply lead to the extension so, while the square footage of the property has increased, the practical gain in space is comparatively small.

Figure 6.12
New works at Compton Verney, based on drawings found in the Soane Museum.

Considering how space and circulation is managed throughout a building should be part of the design process from the outset. The original brief for the Garden Museum suggested a temporary exhibition and gallery space housed in a large pod occupying the middle of the church.

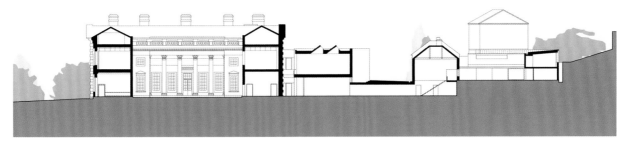

Rather than take this route, Dow Jones Architects suggested that it would be more interesting if the middle of the building was left open for lectures, seminars, debates, film shows and concerts. This came from the realisation that the building has a large volume but comparatively little plan area. The resulting design included a pod for both office use and displays. It was placed in the northwest corner of the church where sunlight produces the least thermal fluctuation, thus providing environmental stability for the exhibits. This left the nave open so not only is the major part of the building's volume retained but it also enables visitors to sit in the open area and appreciate the chancel which, in addition, provides a natural performance and lecture space. This solution also created a permanent exhibition area on top of the pod, currently used for objects associated with the history of gardening, such as spades and other tools.

Improving the visitor experience through better circulation is a requirement of many museums and galleries. At Compton Verney the numerous exhibition spaces were enhanced through careful planning of the flow of space between the three floors of galleries. Glass ramps, bridges and stairs were introduced to link buildings and introduce natural light.

Staircases and lifts

The need to improve circulation and access within a building is often the driving force behind the decision to introduce a staircase or lift. Many factors govern the design of both, not least the need to meet current building regulations. The form that a new staircase takes is dictated by steepness, the rise and going (depth of the tread from front to back), and the headroom available. Many older staircases do not meet modern

Figure 6.13
The open staircase at Astley Castle, Warwickshire.

Figure 6.14
The staircase at St John's College, Oxford, is designed as a piece of free-standing furniture (far left).

Figure 6.15
Glass staircase to the Royal Academy's Sackler Galleries (left).

Figure 6.16
Minimum intervention to
stairs at LSO St Luke's,
Islington.

standards so it is rare that a new staircase can provide an exact replica or fit into a void left by earlier stairs.

Staircases are capable of conjuring a sculptural aesthetic that echoes and reinforces the form of the historic building into which they have been introduced, while being very much of today. This is the case at Tate Britain in London where, as part of a scheme by Caruso St John Architects, circulation spaces around the rotunda at the ground floor, main floor and first floor of the Victorian building were opened up, with a new spiral staircase and lifts connecting all levels. The staircase spirals down from the centre of the domed rotunda, where a surface of monochrome terrazzo recalls the patterned mosaics of the original marble floor.

The challenges associated with introducing staircases into old buildings are illustrated at Astley Castle. Originally, Witherford Watson Mann imagined a sculptural form but the footprint the staircase could occupy was limited, so the geometric constraints on the design were tight. The solution was a timber stud frame with a cranked stringer of steel sandwiched by oak. The components were minimised until there was just enough structural integrity to support the staircase. The oak treads are left hanging with the upper portion braced with ply sheathing to give added rigidity. The half round steel handrail echoes an elegant Georgian style. All the steelwork is painted in a bronze metallic paint.

Wright & Wright Architects took a somewhat similar approach at St John's College, Oxford, when introducing a new staircase to access the Laudian Library from the ground floor at the north end. Extending from a newly created space where existing fabric was retained, the staircase is designed as a piece of free-standing furniture that makes good use of materials: oak, brass, steel and Clipsham stone.

Foster + Partners' insertion of stairs and a lift between the old Burlington House and the Main Galleries at the Royal Academy of Arts ingeniously made use of the 4.25m gap between the two buildings to address the issue of circulation within the Sackler Galleries. The glass stairs and lift seem effortlessly incorporated and have allowed the previously hidden facades to breathe and be appreciated as never before.

When considering where to install a lift at LSO St Luke's, Levitt Bernstein looked at several options, including within the main volume of the church, but this location was rejected because of the need to optimise

acoustics in the principal space and isolate it from all machinery. Other options took into account the condition of the existing staircases at the front of the building. One had retained its roof so the condition of the stairs, the associated panelling and the ironwork was reasonably good. But, with the other, the roof had been lost and with it much of the interior. Consequently, the decision was taken to modify this damaged staircase to install the new lift in its well, making the building more accessible while losing little original fabric.

With the remaining staircases, signs of age were retained wherever possible and clear marks of wear and tear are evident. Despite this, a balance had to be struck between who was using the stairs, frequency of use and the need for safety, so some minimal upgrading was necessary, such as applying non-slip tape to the front of the treads.

Figure 6.17
An opening formed in a
wall at Ditchling Museum,
East Sussex.

POINTS OF INTERVENTION

Internal interventions are potentially more radical that those made externally but are sometimes regarded as secondary. This should not be the case. Junctions within buildings are technical as well as aesthetic elements and require considerable thought. For example, should old segue into new or should there be a clearly defined marker?

At Ditchling Museum there are several clear examples of these carefully considered points of intervention. Where an opening has been formed in the masonry wall, the thickness of the wall is clearly visible. While the cuts of the angle grinder could have been left exposed, it was felt they would appear too harsh, so brick piers were built to contrast with the stonework and delineate the start and end of the opening. The junction is emphasised by the use of CLT installed above; this acts like the proscenium arch in a theatre, creating a layered approach accentuated by a wash of artificial lighting.

External consequences

Internal change may have a visible effect on the exterior of a building and marrying the two is not always easy. Something as simple as the installation of a boiler or ventilation system can result in the unhappy scarring of a facade when it is vented outside. For this reason, thought must be given to all the consequences of a proposed intervention.

From a visual perspective, windows present one of the biggest challenges when internal spaces are divided. This is especially true in churches and other buildings with tall windows where horizontal divisions are necessary to allow for the insertion of floors or a mezzanine. Care needs to be taken to avoid these cutting across windows and creating an intrusive line when viewed from outside.

One design solution is to step the new floor back from the windows so it is less visible externally. This was the route chosen by Wright & Wright Architects at the Longwall Library at Magdalen College, Oxford, where Giles Gilbert Scott had subdivided the capacious interior in the 1930s and added a floor within the high interior space that cut across the building's full-height windows.

Wright & Wright Architects revealed the windows and the true extent of the hall by reinstating its single volume. Into this space bookcases and study areas, split across three levels, were inserted in the

Figure 6.18
The Longwall Library at Magdalen College, Oxford, with windows visible to their full height.

Figure 6.19
Human activity provides
colour inside the National
Theatre.

Figure 6.20
Textures and light within
the Weston Library,
Oxford.

form of a free-standing steel-frame structure encased in oak that stands in the middle, away from the windows. In effect this is one very large piece of furniture, including a new staircase and glass lift, which touches nothing but the floor.

In some schemes, stepping back from the walls and windows needs careful thought as creating a void between the floors below and above may raise issues of internal sound transmission and fire control.

Repetitive fenestration patterns in old buildings also need careful consideration when attempting internal subdivision. Visually, partitions that run directly into windows seldom work internally or externally but, where unavoidable, innovation is called for. One solution sometimes employed is to blank the window so it disappears internally but is retained externally. Usually this involves leaving a black painted void behind the window so, when viewed externally, it appears dark. Where this course is taken it is essential to ensure that the void is sufficiently ventilated and accessible.

SURFACES

Any building changes through time, so in creating something of today the existing surfaces, finishes and materials must be evaluated carefully. At the National Theatre, Denys Lasdun's interiors were architecturally extremely rigorous, with the original foyer areas based on a coherent palette of just five materials: concrete, purple carpet, black engineering floor bricks, stainless steel and dark polished wenge – a tropical hardwood now listed as endangered.

In its regeneration of the theatre, Haworth Tompkins took the decision that these materials should be retained even though the mood they create is somewhat sober, a reflection of the cultural climate in the

1960s and early 1970s. In those decades, the notion of creating a 'cathedral to culture', an austere place to see austere work, would not have seemed incongruous. Lasdun's vision was that human activity would provide the colour and entertainment so that the architecture was deliberately unyielding, and that people were the life and movement running through it.

While up to a point Lasdun's concept works, it does not suit today's audiences and theatre culture. Although none of the finishes and materials have been stripped out, a more transient layer of material has been added on top in the form of modern upholstery and furniture. This has allowed the introduction of colours and textures that lift the mood, making the internal spaces more convivial and friendly than before.

Figure 6.21
Contrasting old and new timber at Wakelins, Suffolk.

Similarly, Wilkinson Eyre's scheme at the Weston Library has introduced new life, bringing back the richness of Giles Gilbert Scott's original decorative scheme, including bronzed screens. To complement this, the internal walls have a wood-float lime-plaster finish that provides texture and tone, a further advantage being that it minimises the need for expansion joints.

Throughout the renovation and extension of Wakelins, James Gorst Architects employed simple, natural finishes to complement the historic oak frame of the Tudor farmhouse. In poor condition and requiring extensive repairs, the existing structure was connected to the extension at ground and first floor levels, with the interior of the former cottages reconfigured to form one large house. Finishes included lime plaster, clay pamments for the floor, slate to line the fireplace opening and oak boards on the walls. In combination, they achieved a look that echoes the past but is undeniably of today. The aesthetic subtly shifts between the old and new parts of the building while still being based on the same material palette but using differently configured and sized components.

ACOUSTICS AND SOUNDPROOFING

Levitt Bernstein's scheme at LSO St Luke's not only addressed the philosophical, structural and aesthetic issues associated with working in the historic environment but also much more practical ones to do with soundproofing and acoustics. With the main space permitting a full symphony orchestra to rehearse, the scheme was designed to exacting acoustic standards, including high-performance glazing, avoidance of noise transmission and variable acoustics.

This was achieved with the help of Chicago-based acoustic designer Kirkegaard Associates, who not only worked with the LSO to ensure the acoustics were right but embraced the need to produce solutions that would be in sympathy with the interior.

By happy coincidence, the rough texture of the existing walls was preferable acoustically to smooth new

Figure 6.22
St Luke's LSO
soundproofing to
windows.

plaster, which would have produced undesirable hard reflections. The old brickwork is slightly absorptive acoustically and partially dampens sound as well as reflecting it in a more diffused way. Additionally, bringing the balconies away from the edge helped define them as new elements but also allowed the sound to move and reverberate around the space, complementing the effect achieved by the walls. A system of retractable banners provides wider control of reverberation, loudness and reflections.

Equally important was the need to soundproof the building to enable broadcast-quality recordings to be made. Attenuating the noise from the busy street immediately outside was no easy task and an extraordinarily high level of sound insulation was required, particularly to the windows. This was complicated by the desire to preserve the entry of natural light into the internal space and minimise the impact of any intervention on the building's external appearance.

Some of the original cast-iron window frames were retained so this dictated the maximum thickness of glass that could be installed in both the existing and the new matching windows. As a consequence, 12 mm laminated glass was employed for all the external glazing. In addition, bespoke secondary glazing containing 50-mm-thick glass was fitted to the face of the wall internally and the frame filled with plaster to create a dense void-free unit. Due to the thickness of the walls, there is a large air gap between the two sets of glazing which provides further soundproofing.

FURNITURE

The intimacy of sitting on a chair, using a table or opening a cupboard is likely to be a richer experience if the piece reflects and embraces the architecture and history of which it is a part. New items of furniture that successfully bridge the gap between old and new tend to combine warmth, texture, tactility and tonality with freshness of design, sensitive use of materials and high-quality workmanship.

Figure 6.23
Furniture and historic colours at Ditchling Museum, East Sussex (right).

Figure 6.24
A CLT refectory table at the Garden Museum, London (far right).

Figure 6.25
New design for the
Weston Library chair.

In the case of Ditchling Museum, architect Adam Richards and the museum director met suppliers and manufacturers and selected furniture together. The colour palette for the furniture and the interiors connects directly with the museum's subject matter: Eric Gill, the artist and typographer associated with the Arts and Crafts movement. The pamphlets he disseminated were generally white pages with black text and often featured red motifs so black, red and white became the dominant colours of the interior.

The chairs that were chosen were produced by a company that specialises in designing and making craft furniture and were painted red. Three-legged stools were selected as they are almost identical to a typographer's work stool exhibit within the museum.

Other items at Ditchling Museum, such as the reception desk and the shelves in the shop, were fashioned from remnants of CLT left over from the building work, providing a point of crossover within the interior, so old and new timber furniture are encountered side by side.

At the Garden Museum, architect Alun Jones was responsible for helping design the furniture. Again CLT was used, this time to create tables that would continue the character of the new structure. These were designed so they could be configured to run the whole length of the nave, allowing visitors and groups to sit together.

In some cases it is essential to create bespoke furniture, for example to fit within the curved walls of Martello Tower Y, where the fittings and finishes

Figure 6.26
Altar and furniture at
Beeston Parish Church,
Nottingham.

throughout are largely bespoke and selected and installed with great attention to detail.

Responding to modern and historic interiors calls for a diversity of styles. The bespoke furniture, created in a collaboration between Eric Parry Architects and furniture designer Matthew Marchbank, provided the Holburne Museum in Bath with benches made of ammonia-fumed oak (a process that both darkens the oak and brings out the grain) and with a brown-and-black horsehair seat pad. These discreet pieces offer a place of rest within the exhibition spaces. The collaboration also resulted in several bench designs for St Martin-in-the-Fields, using the same materials.

In Oxford, Bodleian Libraries have a history of commissioning bespoke furniture, and a chair design competition resulted in new reading room chairs for the Weston Library. Designed by Edward Barber and Jay Osgerby with manufacturer Isokon.

'You're never starting cold, you're coming in at a certain point in history and, although the furniture is new and different, I try to sit quietly in the background with my work. I also try to avoid novelty because things are only novel once and you can soon tire of that sort of thing. Nor is it necessarily classical, it emerges from one man's hands with all the foibles and interests of that person. The timber is solid, there is no pastiche of materials, there is no MDF being called walnut.'

Nicholas Hobbs, furniture maker

Figure 6.27
The Lady Chapel Altar, Ely Cathedral.

Plus, the three-legged oak chair is a response to the brief which combined a strong sense of craft heritage, sculptural form and complex reader requirements.

A similar balance of the traditional and the modern was achieved with the furniture in the Members Room at Tate Britain, where Caruso St John Architects introduced tables and seating inspired by leading British Arts and Crafts designers active in 1897, the founding year of the gallery. This includes an asymmetric armchair by Edwin Lutyens.

The Arts and Crafts tradition is well suited to new church furniture, as exemplified in the work of designer and furniture maker Nicholas Hobbs. The altar, presidential and side chairs and lectern of oak and ebony he crafted for the nave sanctuary of Beeston Parish Church, Nottingham, were installed as part of a major refurbishment of the building. The ensemble exudes honesty and an overwhelming impression of understated classic simplicity.

The Gothic language of the church, which although medieval was largely rebuilt by George Gilbert Scott in the 1840s, is recalled in the arches of the altar table. Liturgy and symbolism also play their part: through-tenons on the arms of the chairs are a tactile element that, when pressed under the hand, leave the imprint of a cross on the palm.

Hobbs has similarly tied his work at Lincoln Cathedral to the building. The congregational chairs reflect Norman detailing on the west front: the backs feature zigzag-figured oak grain and a projecting maple radius profile. In the east end of the building, the altar is purely Gothic with multiple interlocking curves. Importantly, the oak was sourced from two forests in areas of France relevant to the life of St Hugh, who rebuilt the cathedral and in whose chapel the furniture stands.

Rarely are additions to church interiors as striking as the wrought-iron screen and altar table below the main east window of the Lady Chapel at Ely Cathedral. Designed by John Maddison, a Cambridgeshire-based artist and expert on medieval architecture, the work is cleverly arranged to show off the remains of an early fourteenth century reredos carved into the chapel wall. While obviously of today, the screen has a strongly medieval character and is complemented by a new altar. This is made of oak and is fronted by a gilded steel sheet embellished with water-cut lettering.

Figure 6.28
The Instruments of the Passion reredos, Bishop Alcock's Chapel, Ely Cathedral.

John Maddison was also responsible for the design of the Instruments of the Passion reredos in Bishop Alcock's Chapel at Ely Cathedral, installed in 2004. This is formed of marine-ply panels within an oak frame that incorporates simplified Gothic mouldings. The panels are painted in oil with a geometric design and illustrate some of the Instruments of the Passion using locally sourced artefacts: the hammer is from Maddison's own toolbox, the nails are from the cathedral roof and the sword was found in the bed of the nearby River Ouse.

Figure 6.29
The raw rock face forms the rear wall of the Copper Kingdom Centre, Anglesey.

CURATING SPACES

Spaces within old buildings frequently tell stories that can add value to new design. In its scheme for Southwark Cathedral, Richard Griffiths Architects linked the new buildings to the cathedral by creating a glass-covered internal 'street' echoing the line of a Victorian alley. Along this street further links to the past include the gravelled surface of a Roman road, the Saxon foundations of the early church and the medieval remains of a seventeenth century pottery kiln.

Artefacts that were present in an original building can form a sculptural focal point, as exemplified at the Thomas Homes development of the Old Railway Quarter in Swindon. In the entrance hall to one of the converted buildings a redundant works machine pays tribute to the site's railway heritage. There is no attempt to recreate or delete the past, instead the machinery is presented as an elegant exhibit, sitting on a plinth of modern engineering bricks and surrounded by an evidently new tubular steel-and-glass screen.

'With Ditchling Museum we were able to design spaces that had a very clear identity of their own. We were dealing with buildings that weren't being used for their original function so there was something quite enjoyable about being able to invent stories for the new spaces that draw both on the history of the building and on the stories of the artists whose work is in the collection.'

Adam Richards, Adam Richards Architects

Within the Copper Kingdom Centre a direct link with the building's heritage exists in the rear wall, a rock face. Despite the structural engineer's initial advice that this should be entirely covered with a steel mat, it was retained following a painstaking analysis and careful consolidation of areas that might cause concern. The retention of the natural rock face has allowed a direct connection to the material the industry was based on and provides the main focus for the visitor experience within the building. The rock wall is in effect an exhibit, revealing in its patina, colour and texture where the copper ore was tipped down into the bin – it still retains the iron tackle that originally held the ropes and pulleys used by the workers to go up and down. The sound of water dripping from the rock and the juxtaposition of the natural cliff face to the internal space allows the visitor a brief hint of life underground, and reinforces the interpretive displays which illustrate the exhibition.

Figure 6.30
Ditchling Museum cart lodge interior, with numbered features.

An equally radical approach was taken at Ditchling Museum within the cart lodge that now forms the entrance. The space within was conceived as the museum's first exhibit and was opened up internally by removing the first floor and exposing the roof structure. This presents an open volume that resembles an exploded drawing, thanks to a collaboration with a graphic designer who numbered the parts and keyed them to information on a paddle that visitors can hold. By allowing the building to be read in this way the different aspects of the structure are easily understood and a connection is provided with the past. A further link to the building is maintained through the paddle's handle, which is made from recycled timber.

CHAPTER 7:
FIT FOR THE FUTURE

Buildings are constantly evolving. Daily use, subtle movement, alterations or additions, coupled with the patination and decay of surfaces through wear and weather, are all part of this process. For a building to occupy its future place successfully, each of these elements must be considered alongside the needs of today.

The goal for those living and working with old buildings must be to create and maintain structures and places that are accessible, enjoyable, comfortable and sustainable. In fulfilling these aims, challenges and dilemmas abound.

Traditional skills and materials should be cherished and embraced but new technology and thinking must not be discounted. Many in the past would undoubtedly have adopted modern techniques, such as computer numerical control (CNC) for cutting materials, had they been available. That said, while new technology allows us to reproduce detail or even entire structures very accurately, it must be used with care as it can never recapture the spirit of the original, which is the product of ageing and generations of change.

Life and honesty of purpose are essential ingredients of successful buildings of all ages. While redefining the function of some old buildings may be hard, it is a challenge that must be met. Only by making buildings fit for the future and engaging with cultural, social and economic realities can we ensure their sustainability and survival. Sustainability is an overworked term but, in this context, is used to describe a diverse range of issues, from access to energy efficiency. All buildings will have to adapt to climate change and any interventions made today must take into account the impact extreme weather events may have on structures and materials.

Figure 7.00
Flood protection barriers in Wakefield (left).

Figure 7.01
The Clerkenwell Cooperage, London, where the historic qualities of the former brewery have been retained in the residential conversion (right).

In improving the resilience of historic buildings, energy efficiency, flood defences, overheating and indoor air quality rank high among the issues to consider but must be matched by a determination to maintain the vital qualities that make old buildings special. In so doing, it is worth recalling the words of William Morris: '*We are only trustees for those who come after us*'.

ACCESSIBILITY

Providing inclusive access to buildings through good design must always be the goal. This benefits everyone, extending far beyond those with mobility issues or other disabilities. No individual is immune from having a need that makes access difficult at some point, be it due to age, pregnancy, temporary injury, pushing a baby's buggy or carrying heavy or difficult loads.

Finding solutions is about more than installing ramps. For example, people with visual impairment may be helped by utilising modern interpretations of some of the characteristics that make old buildings special: colour, texture and light. The degree to which this can be achieved has to be carefully judged, with temporary arrangements avoided wherever possible and preference given to good permanent solutions that will serve for the long term. The first principle of addressing access issues associated with old buildings is to consider the architectural opportunities and ways of enhancing the experience so users are able to interact in a logical, comfortable way.

Even a building as recent as the National Theatre, which opened in 1976, poses a number of challenges when considering access. The fluidity and complexity that excited the theatre's original architect, Denys Lasdun – and other architects working in the 1960s and 1970s with concrete structures – required many voids, split levels and staircases. This resulted in a building that was largely inaccessible, to the extent that even the main restaurant could not be accessed by a lift. Haworth Tompkins successfully solved these problems in its scheme for the building, completed in 2015, but not without having to overcome major challenges in balancing the needs of the building with those of its users.

An extensive refurbishment of the 1917 HM Treasury building in London completed by Foster + Partners in 2002, included significantly improved access through the installation of external ramps. The existing steps leading up to the main entrance of the Grade II listed building were brought forward to a landing and ramped access was provided from both sides, creating a symmetrical arrangement of ramp and steps that complements the historic facade.

'You have to ask fundamental questions about how you are going to find the building, where you want to enter the building, what the experience of finding the building and entering the building is going to be like. Then you have to think about how you get around the building both horizontally and vertically. It's a fantastically intricate and fascinating architectural challenge.'

Richard Griffiths, Richard Griffiths Architects

Figure 7.02
New access ramp to HM
Treasury, London.

Figure 7.03
Southwark Cathedral,
entrance to the north
transept.

Within the Garden Museum, reorganisation of the entrance made full regulatory compliance possible and the installation of a lift provided access to the upper level of the building. Access to the toilets was more problematic and only fully resolved with the second phase of the project, which allowed floor levels to be rationalised. This saw the numerous changes of level that had developed over time reduced to just two by building up the floor to create a level nave and chancel, with the junction between the two evened out.

A similar method was employed by Communion Architects within St Andrew's Church. Here the access was subtly upgraded through the installation of a suspended floor in oak to create a uniformly level surface. This allows everyone to enter and use the whole building.

Many projects are predicated on access and require an integrated approach. This was the case for Richard Griffiths Architects' scheme at Southwark Cathedral, where access was key to developing a sensible and pleasant system of circulation. It saw the creation of a major accessible entrance for the cathedral from the Thames footpath and via the Millennium Courtyard that evokes the monastic cloisters formerly on the site. This includes a 1-in-20 ramp and a platform lift.

Ramps

Access is generally a permanent requirement so it is reasonable to create a solution with this in mind. Generally there are two approaches, especially when constructing ramps: either build out into the void or build into the solid structure – the first solution may be preferred as there will be much less intrusion and damage to the fabric of the building.

Generally the longer the ramp, the less obvious it is. The potential danger with this approach is that it may result in a larger amount of historic fabric being covered, damaged or lost. At St Albans Cathedral, Richard Griffiths Architects undertook a scheme to make every part of the 165m long Abbey Church accessible to all. One of the aisles is little used, so it can accommodate a ramp some 10m long without it being a problem visually as it appears to be just a sloping section of floor.

Level access was an integral part of Wright & Wright Architects' landscaping of the quadrangle leading to the reworked Longwall Library at Magdalen College, Oxford. Incorporated in the outside space is a gently sloping ramp which weaves down through raised stone beds that contain planting. This integrates perfectly with the new reading room that extends out to one side and, as well as serving its purpose to provide access, is a relaxing space to be enjoyed in its own right.

Purcell's refurbishment of Kew Palace in Richmond, Surrey, involved considerable work to improve accessibility to the building, which is both Grade I listed and a Scheduled Monument. Built in the 17th century as a merchant's house, it served as a home to George II's daughters and as a school for the future king, George III, later becoming his private retreat in Kew Gardens. For its history to be understood, it was important to create an accessible route around the building.

The decision was taken to move the ticket desks and shop to a 1930s building outside the palace. This enabled the front door to appear domestic and uncluttered while allowing visitors to approach the palace along the same route as would have been taken by visitors arriving by carriage in earlier times.

Portland stone steps led up to the front door. In order to retain these while providing easy access, a simple ramp of stone slabs, delineated by a low brick wall, was constructed to run alongside the front of the building, leading to and building into the side of the original steps. In addition, to create a level threshold to the door, the steps were carefully dismantled and the landing at the top raised by inserting a stone band. The potential intrusion of handrails in front of the building's aesthetically sensitive front facade was avoided by detailing the gradient of the ramp so they would be unnecessary.

Figure 7.04
Ramps within the Longwall quad at Magdalen College, Oxford.

Figure 7.05
Ramp access to Kew Palace.

Lifts

Within Kew Palace there was a need to provide full access to the ground and first floors. Installing a lift within the building was impossible but, through research, Purcell found that there had once been an eighteenth century wooden water closet shaft on the outside of the building's west elevation. There was thus a precedent for a full-height structure in a suitable location for a lift shaft. It also meant that openings that had previously been blocked up could be reopened and become the access route into the lift.

As well as responding to the original closet's siting, the new shaft's crisp exterior of lapped oak weatherboarding and traditional leadwork echoes its visual simplicity. With the footprint of the lift dictated by archaeological evidence of the size of the privy shaft, and the need for the addition to have appropriate visual scale in the context of the palace, it was necessary for Purcell to design and engineer a totally bespoke solution in conjunction with the lift manufacturer.

The final design has the shaft sitting on a brick plinth that follows the pronounced plinth at the base of the palace building. This serves as the lift pit, the depth of which was restricted by the retained archaeology. A further challenge was avoiding the decorative pediment of the palace's facade so it was necessary to step the top of the structure back to be clear of the brickwork.

The Kew Palace scheme enabled the use of the building's undercroft as a learning centre. The archaeology prevented the external lift continuing down to this level so, instead, a separate platform lift was installed inconspicuously just behind it.

Figure 7.06
The external lift shaft at
Kew Palace.

In a public building, where there are more than three or four steps, platform lifts are often the answer. In comparison, chair or stairlifts tend to be visually intrusive, and may involve more fixings into the historic fabric than a platform lift, although they sometimes provide access when it is impossible to accommodate a vertical lift. For wheelchair users, stairlifts also necessitate transferring from one chair to another and require the wheelchair to be transported separately to the next level.

Work at St Albans Cathedral required the insertion of a platform lift in an archaeologically sensitive location. The lift permits entry to the chapel containing the shrine of St Alban, where a flight of four steps previously prevented wheelchair access. Lateral thinking was needed in understanding how best to incorporate the lift and, although various access options were considered, it was decided that the most suitable solution architecturally was, counter-intuitively, also the most prominent. Bold and permanent, it involved the construction of low flanking walls and a new stone platform and ceremonial steps in the retroquire. The scissor mechanism of the lift has a very shallow pit sitting above sensitive archaeology, which was fully recorded.

A somewhat similar approach was taken at Ditchling Museum, where, within the link building between the cart lodge entrance and the gallery space, there are stairs with a platform lift alongside, partly concealed behind a raised and deliberately 'presented' slab of CLT. Similarly discreet is the solution chosen at Astley Castle, where a platform lift has been installed to provide an alternative means of access to the main living area on the upper floor. This was introduced through the retained medieval shaft of the spiral stair and it makes its ascent between aged wall surfaces.

Figure 7.07
A platform lift within St Albans Cathedral (right).

Figure 7.08
Service and access lift at Astley Castle, Warwickshire (far right).

LIGHTING

Few buildings are more associated with matters of lighting than theatres. At the National Theatre the original aim had been to try to recreate a kind of candlelit glow within the foyers so that people looking in from the outside would appear to be viewing a cave-like space. Early photographs show the beauty of this and the attractive way the light revealed the texture of the bare concrete. But it was also dark and the audience had difficulty reading their programmes. Consequently, in the 1990s, it was replaced with lighting that was much brighter, but harsh and less sympathetic to the original building.

In its 2015 scheme, Haworth Tompkins has returned to the mood of Lasdun's lighting, trusting his instinct. The new lighting retains the sober quality of the original and tries to achieve a candlelit warmth. In conjunction with this, one element of the lighting has seen suspended coloured tubes introduced into the large triple-height foyer spaces. This bolder lighting, like the new furniture and upholstery, is transient, so can be replaced to reflect changing times, and provides light and colour in a way that warms the foyers and makes them more welcoming than they were before.

Lighting old buildings sympathetically frequently presents huge challenges. The refurbishment of the Oxford University Museum of Natural History provided the opportunity to undertake a major relighting project and change a space that was poorly lit and too dark to use at night into one that was attractive, exciting and offered a wide range of uses. At the same time the project posed the problem of how to integrate and install the necessary equipment within the distinctive Grade I listed neo-Gothic building.

Built in 1860, the museum's main structural beams and columns were made from cast iron and are an integral part of its architecture. Drilling into these or having highly visible luminaires and cabling was not desirable so the team behind the project devised an ingenious solution using bespoke magnetic brackets.

With previous experience of using magnets to fix exhibits, Oxford University's Ashmolean Museum manufactured 2,542 magnet mounts using 8,056 specialist magnets sourced from the aircraft industry.

Three types of luminaires were employed, carefully chosen to minimise

Figure 7.09
Lighting in the National Theatre foyer.

Figure 7.10
The new lighting scheme in the Oxford University Museum of Natural History.

Figure 7.11
Uplighters at the Oxford
University Museum of
Natural History (right).

Figure 7.12
Concealed lighting
accentuating the handrail
and brickwork in Martello
Tower Y (far right).

visual intrusion. Two provide up and downlighting on the columns and arches while the third design creates a focal point as a modern representation of the original gas chandeliers that still hang from the museum's roof. All the LED lamps are dimmable and are networked to a lighting control system that includes colour changing capabilities.

The success of the project means the museum is able to stay open for longer and, by selecting from the many lighting scenes that may be created, a huge range of special events can be held, increasing revenues and providing a better experience for visitors.

Another difficult-to-light interior was Martello Tower Y in Suffolk. Here uplighters and discreet, hidden lighting serve to define the sculptural interior of vaulted brickwork and the form of the curving roof extension, while supplementing the available natural light.

SERVICES

With old buildings it is vital to develop an overall strategy for integrating services from the outset and, except on very small projects, employing an independent consultant mechanical and electrical engineer will be an asset. Maintaining a good dialogue between the designer, the M&E (Mechanical and Electrical) consultant and the contractors and sub-contractors throughout the project is essential. Inevitably there is a balancing act between achieving the best for the fabric and introducing the services necessary for the building's long-term functionality.

While service routes can be discovered and plotted on drawings, there is great value in conducting visual inspections on site. This approach frequently reveals fresh possibilities for installing cable and pipe runs inconspicuously and with minimum damage to the fabric. This can include identifying opportunities to run a cable along the edge or within the shape of a moulding which may not immediately be apparent on a plan. Additionally, the careful positioning of service boxes and outlets can help reduce visible cable runs or the need to cut through historic fabric.

Chasing into original fabric should be avoided if at all possible. In some cases it is better to be totally honest about the presence of services, either running them in a well-detailed surface conduit or in cable trays suspended from the ceiling. Many old buildings have voids; at the SPAB headquarters in London, cabling was carefully inserted behind eighteenth century panelling without its removal. The most common voids are disused flues. These frequently offer service routes for ventilation ducting, pipework and cabling but care must be taken to install relevant fire stops, soundproofing and thermal insulation.

Specifying and planning service routes can consume a considerable amount of design time. Costs may escalate if better-quality fittings are required and from the extra care that has to be taken during installation if services are on show. For example, cables and pipes need to be precisely aligned without kinks or blemishes. Sizing is also important: a heating engineer may specify pipes of different diameters but visually they are likely to look better if they are all of the same size. In such cases there is likely to be a trade-off between performance and aesthetics, so the project's aims and competing priorities must be carefully considered. Well-designed and carefully installed systems will be more robust and require less maintenance over time.

Access is always an important consideration when planning and installing services but particularly in old buildings, where future damage to fabric must be minimised. Where necessary, access hatches should be fitted to enable maintenance and inspection of pipes, cables, ducts and flues and to provide for the possibility of adding further services in the future should the need arise.

Ideally, any fixings or small penetrations for pipes or cables should be made into or through the mortar of joints as this is relatively easily repaired in the future should changes or removal be necessary. A hole drilled into brick or stonework is irreversible. Where additions are being made, services may sometimes be integrated within the new elements of the building rather than the old. This is the case at LSO St Luke's where they have been installed through the floor slab and balconies. At the Garden Museum the use of CLT had the benefit of allowing much of the electrical cabling to be attached to the back of the panels or run in a void space between two panels.

Within the Copper Kingdom Centre, all services, including heating, IT systems and electrical cabling, are contained in the new timber floor deck and the walls of the pods that represent the original chutes. These also accommodate unobtrusive heating ventilation grilles.

As the relighting of the Oxford University Museum of Natural History demonstrates, it is possible to install over 4 km of cabling discreetly within an important listed building without causing damage. One of the secrets was the use of magnets to secure the cabling in place but the success of the project was also due to the careful routing of the cables and, where necessary, painting them to blend in with the surface colour of the cast-iron structure. Control of the system by museum staff is entirely wireless.

'Chances to incorporate services are often there if you look for them. We're not pretending they don't exist or hiding them away but, at the same time, we don't want them to be the first thing you see.'

Gary Tidmarsh, Levitt Bernstein

Figure 7.14
A battery-free wireless
light switch – energy is
generated with each use.

Wireless control systems – ranging from light switches and heating thermostats to more complex building management systems – potentially offer a cost-effective way of reducing the need to install cable runs that may be both unsightly and cause damage to historic fabric. A potential drawback is the thick walls and large chimney breasts in some older buildings that can block or interfere with communication between devices.

The installation of radiators in old buildings always poses dilemmas about style and position and, where they are required, careful thought has to be given to their integration. One solution is to install them in the redundant fireplaces as this is where the heat source would originally have been and their intrusiveness is minimised. Some upgrades, such as fire detection, alarm and suppression systems and emergency lighting, may be necessary and unavoidable due to statutory controls. As with all services, installation should be treated as sensitively as possible. The aim is to provide appropriate and reliable protection, but this need not necessarily require the equipment to be intrusive, provided the relevant standards are met. Careful choice of systems, consideration of cable runs and discussion with the authority responsible for providing certification is beneficial. With the installation of all services, fire stopping of holes through which smoke or flames can pass is essential, including within trunking and switchgear.

ADDRESSING SUSTAINABILITY

Incorporating environmental and sustainability measures into buildings is an essential part of good design and allows new work to reinvigorate the old so that historic structures will continue to stand the test of time. Successful schemes frequently embrace factors beyond the day-to-day performance of the building. For example, the new stone walls that extend the White House on the Isle of Coll, in the Hebrides, were created from recycled rubble from the site; this reduced transportation and environmental impact since the use of imported aggregate and masonry was kept to a minimum.

The effect buildings have on the landscape is illustrated by Hunsett Mill, which stands in the heart of the Norfolk Broads, a man-made wetland sustained through human intervention and the building of water-pumping mills, dykes and canals.

Hunsett Mill became redundant when wind power gave way to electric pumps. In undertaking the new scheme to replace many years of poorly executed extensions to the original mill keeper's house with a single new extension, the architects, Acme, were determined to embrace the emphasis placed on conservation and a managed return to nature within the landscape of the Broads.

Removal of the poorly executed, piecemeal accretions reduced past conflict with the local flood ecology and allowed future flood risk to be addressed through the construction of a new embankment at the back of the site. This offers more reliability and efficiency than previous downstream defences and also returns 25 hectares of nearby forest and grassland to pre-industrial marshland conditions. To enhance the local ecology, indigenous plants have been used within the garden. Site damage during the construction of the new extension was mitigated through careful design and material choices that reduced the amount of heavy machinery required.

Figure 7.15
The conserved setting of Hunsett Mill, Norfolk.

Increasingly, green or living roofs are employed to merge landscape and structure while helping to reduce the water run-off from buildings, filter pollutants, increase biodiversity and provide a habitat for wildlife. Aesthetically, green roofs soften the appearance of buildings, and, as in the case of Astley Castle, have the added design benefits of protecting roof coverings from the sun and improving thermal and acoustic insulation.

Figure 7.16
Green roof on part of Astley Castle, Warwickshire.

ENERGY EFFICIENCY

One of the greatest challenges relating to old buildings is energy efficiency: in the UK, buildings contribute 43 per cent of all carbon emissions, of which more than half come from homes. Cutting emissions is crucial but, when considering how an old building should be made more energy efficient, the initial consideration is the same as when contemplating any change. It necessitates being clear about the elements of the building that make it special and significant.

Once this is understood there should be a sense of how these factors relate to the building's environmental characteristics. The building or elements within it may already be contributing positively and any scheme resulting in change must not undermine the structure's existing performance characteristics, ruin its carbon status or jeopardise its future.

Figure 7.17
Sustainability strategies at
LSO St Luke's, Islington.

Solutions such as those devised by engineers Max Fordham for LSO St Luke's give an indication of the range of measures that might be employed to create an energy-efficient strategy. These maximise the entry of daylight through large windows, glazed walls and rooflights, while the danger of overheating is attenuated by the building's thermal mass, natural ventilation through the old bell tower that exploits wind energy and the use of trees for shading. Other measures include green roof constructions and the use of energy from the ground to provide heating and cooling.

Energy-efficient retrofits

With 80 per cent of the buildings that will be used in the UK in the year 2050 already built, the need to retrofit old buildings so they are energy efficient and sustainable is clear and urgent. Before any work can start, the knock-on effect of each action must be considered. This is particularly important when considering interventions such as the installation of thermal insulation or draughtproofing, since the use of inappropriate or incompatible techniques or materials may result in unintended consequences, including damp, decay, beetle attack, mould and poor indoor air quality.

External wall insulation potentially results in the loss of architectural features, texture and patina of age, thereby totally changing the appearance of a building and indeed whole street scenes. The installation of new windows and doors can be equally damaging both aesthetically and in terms of loss of original fabric. Many windows are unnecessarily removed and sent to landfill when secondary glazing and other measures could be successfully employed to improve the energy efficiency of the originals.

A layer of insulation added to the internal face of a wall may not only result in the loss of features but can also contribute to the formation of interstitial condensation – the condensation of internal water vapour when it meets the cool wall surface. In this scenario, there may be concerns relating to moisture damage and degradation, particularly at wall surfaces and joist ends.

Moisture building up within the structure is not just a threat to the health of the building's fabric, it is a very real danger to the health of the building's occupants. A moist environment provides the ideal conditions for dust mites, mould and bacteria, which can cause allergic reactions and other health problems. These issues will not be identified in simple computer models and may not be obvious in buildings for several years, by which time the problem will be far advanced.

Natural insulation materials may help address these issues. For example, the makeup of wood-fibre insulation means the moisture that forms in the insulation is returned to the room via capillary action and the hygroscopicity of the breathable material, thereby avoiding potential structural and health hazards. Wall

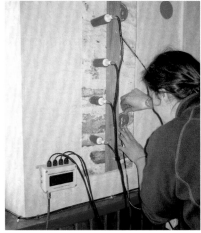

Figure 7.18
Natural wood-fibreboard insulation being applied to internal walls (far left).

Figure 7.19
Data gathering for the SPAB's energy-efficiency research (left).

insulation is generally not the primary method of improving energy efficiency. In most cases, other options should be considered first, such as loft insulation, overhauling windows, secondary glazing and eliminating draughts. There is no doubt that older buildings can frequently benefit from sensitive, well-informed energy-efficiency measures but a full assessment of the proposed retrofitting scheme should always be undertaken before it is executed so that ways can be found to improve performance without compromising fabric or character. This means that those surveying properties and specifying retrofit solutions must be skilled in understanding both the building and the full impact of the measures proposed. The way the building is to be occupied and used must also be considered. Regular maintenance and ongoing monitoring should be a prerequisite for any retrofit scheme to ensure any problems that emerge are identified promptly and that lessons learnt are disseminated effectively.

Research

Older houses are often vilified for their poor thermal performance but research shows that the standard U-value calculations, used across the construction industry, significantly underestimate the thermal performance of traditional solid walls in the majority of cases. The research, by bodies including the SPAB, is a revelation because accepted theoretical performance figures have long been used as a standard base measurement when buildings are being upgraded or altered.

Ultimately this underestimation of the performance of solid walls could have negative consequences for older buildings as it might lead to disproportionate and misguided energy-saving interventions being adopted. Given that traditional buildings in the UK number in the millions, the potential for damage and ineffective measures is huge. By using the new evidential data and gaining a better understanding of the way old buildings perform, unnecessary and invasive measures can be avoided, saving potentially harmful and costly work.

DAYLIGHTING

Natural light in buildings is beneficial to health and reduces energy loads, but introducing daylight when adapting and extending old buildings sometimes presents challenges. Punching new window openings in historic fabric is rarely acceptable and some structures, such as mills and warehouses, have deep floorplates that will require innovative design solutions in order to ensure the availability of natural light and ventilation.

When undertaking the conversion of Martello Tower Y on the Suffolk coast, a major concern for Piercy&Company was how to introduce light into the structure. Early on the decision was taken to create an upside-down house with the living area at the top so it could benefit from new rooflights and windows. Providing light to the lower parts of the building was more challenging as, due to the building's scheduled status, no new window openings could be created to serve the bedrooms, bathrooms and utility areas in the basement. The problem was resolved by splaying the existing window openings internally – leaving the external appearance unaltered – and drilling six 450 mm holes using a diamond core bit just inside the window sills, down through 4.5m of fully bonded brickwork, to create light pipes opening into the basement. The window sill over the top of the shaft was replaced with glass. A further link with the outside was achieved by drilling small holes through the external wall to create a camera obscura effect that allows the landscape outside to be projected within the bedroom.

Sun tubes or sun pipes are useful for bringing natural light into buildings, particularly when dealing with internal bathrooms and windowless hallways. Light is gathered from a roof or wall-mounted fitting and this then passes down through the building via a highly reflective pipe to a ceiling fitting below. These systems have the advantage that their installation generally causes minimal structural damage as they can usually be fitted between rafters and joists without the need for the existing timber to be cut.

Figure 7.20
Light cores introduced at Martello Tower Y, Suffolk.

Even where highly efficient energy-saving lighting is available, it should be carefully controlled so maximum use is made of daylight. Following the relighting of the Oxford University Museum of Natural History, day-to-day operation of the new LED lighting system is fully automated with control linked to a sophisticated, roof-mounted device that constantly monitors the amount and direction of available daylight through photocell and infrared sensors.

Bringing light into the circulation areas was one of the key design objectives within the Royal Academy of Arts' Sackler Galleries. Previously, the space had acted as a light well between two buildings so translucent glazing has been introduced to much of the floor area, as well as along one side of the reception, allowing in both direct and diffuse light. This has combined an open-air feeling with a general sense of luminosity.

Bath's Holburne Museum similarly makes the most of daylight. Not only does the glass extension play with light and reflection externally, it ensures daylighting to the café and, where required, allows light deep into the interior exhibition space, helped by voids in the mezzanine inserted within the new building.

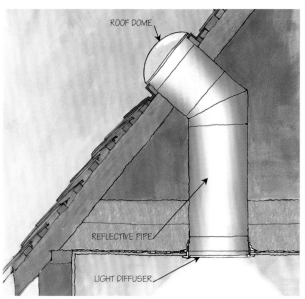

ROOF DOME

REFLECTIVE PIPE

LIGHT DIFFUSER

Figure 7.21
Sun pipes allow natural light to be brought into buildings.

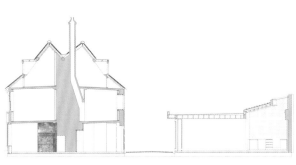

Extensive glazing is also used at the Thermae Bath Spa complex in Bath to draw daylight deep into the building; where it is necessary to safeguard the privacy of bathers, circular glass lenses and translucent panels are employed.

Within the domestic setting, the importance of designing the building envelope and interior layout to exploit natural light to full potential is illustrated at Tanners Hill, in Deptford. A light well and small courtyard created at the heart of the house, together with a rooflight above the kitchen, subtly introduce daylight and a sense of space.

Solar gain and overheating

On a global scale, more energy is used to keep buildings cool than to heat them. One of the benefits of many old buildings is that the thermal mass of the brick, stone or other heavyweight materials used in their construction absorbs, stores and then releases heat over time. This thermal buffering is increasingly important as temperatures vary in more extreme ways due to climate change since it helps moderate the effects of summer overheating and, in colder weather, means that any solar gain or warmth from heating systems is retained.

Once the heat from the sun penetrates a building, it is hard to expel, so devices such as external folding or sliding shutters are an ideal means of reducing the potential for overheating, although they rely on human or automated operation. New interpretations of traditional techniques offer effective means of preventing solar gain reaching interiors. Mole Architects employed frameless glazing and insulated shutters to provide both privacy and shading to their extension of Ramblers cottage, while creating a lively facade. Roofs with wide eaves are another way to provide shading from high summer sun while allowing the entry of lower winter sun. A traditional interpretation of a brise soleil is a pergola over which is grown a deciduous climber.

This offers summer shading but allows in low winter light after the leaves have fallen. Strategically placed deciduous trees may be employed in a similar way, although care must be taken to avoid root damage to buildings. Attic rooms are particularly prone to overheating and this is a concern when undertaking conversions. The correct choice of insulation material is vital, with materials such as wood fibre restricting the ingress of summer heat by buffering, through a process called phase shift or heat decrement delay. This slows the heat's progress by absorbing it during the hottest parts of the day so that it can become a positive source of heat when the building is cooler at night.

VENTILATION

The large volume of air capable of moving through an old building is easily illustrated by watching the smoke from an open fire emanate from its chimney. As airtightness in buildings is improved, this natural ventilation is diminished, consequently effective controlled ventilation becomes ever more important to avoid poor indoor air quality that can affect health, wellbeing and productivity. Introducing ventilation into schemes involving old buildings is not always straightforward. Having already demonstrated innovation in bringing natural light into its Martello Tower Y project, Piercy&Company utilised 200-mm-diameter holes drilled through the substantial brickwork of the structure to accommodate the supply and exhaust ducts of the Mechanical Ventilation with Heat Recovery (MVHR) system in the basement and ground floors. Ducts also provided routes for gas, electricity and water supplies to the kitchen and for heating the roof.

Reworking Magdalen College's Longwall Library presented even greater challenges. These included overheating and problems relating to the busy road outside, where traffic lights cause traffic to constantly stop and start. This meant that the building's windows on the street side could not be opened because of the unacceptable levels of pollution and noise.

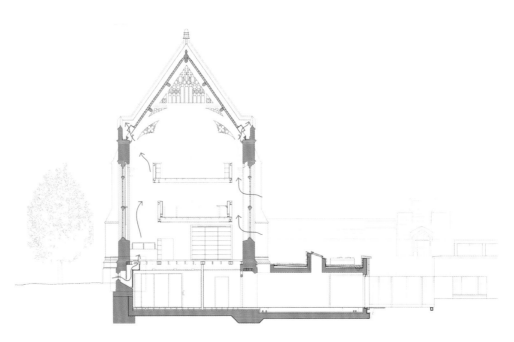

Figure 7.25
The passive ventilation system at Magdalen College's Longwall Library.

Wright & Wright Architects worked with engineers Max Fordham to create a passive ventilation strategy that involved minimum intervention to the listed building. Air intake is through motorised lower-ground-floor windows via a chamber (plenum) that is designed to absorb noise and pollutants and, on the quadrangle side, through opening windows. From here the air passes naturally upwards within the library's interior and out through the original filigree-pattern roof vents that date from a time when ventilation was required for gas lighting. Again, an attenuated plenum has been introduced, together with top-hung motorised vents, just above the lead gutter and hidden by the building's castellated stone parapet.

Much simpler is the ventilation within the non-heated common parts at the Old Railway Quarter in Swindon. Here, windows that were beyond repair were replaced with simple glass screens that allow air to freely flow around the edges while providing some protection against the weather and a view out to an inner courtyard. Clearly such a solution would be less suitable in exposed locations suffering wind-driven rain.

Figure 7.26
Spaced glass panes at the Old Railway Quarter, Swindon, allowing natural ventilation while providing security.

ENERGY GENERATION

Photovoltaic (PV) and solar thermal panels are often seen as a scar on the roofs of old buildings, though features such as parapets on houses or castellation on churches may allow them to be screened from sight. At the Old Railway Quarter, thoughtful design means that, while they are visible, their impact has been minimised. In all, 177 PV panels have been installed to power communal areas and, by positioning them in line with the newly inserted rooflights, they have a unified appearance that suits the industrial nature of the building.

Heat pumps are increasingly used in the context of old buildings. At Compton Verney, a heat pump extracts energy from the lake and supplies underfloor heating in the environmentally controlled galleries. Offering the advantage of being largely out of sight, ground-source heat pumps can work well in the context of old buildings where major works are being undertaken and there is the opportunity to drill boreholes or dig the trenches necessary for the long loops of pipes required, although it is important to be aware of the possibility of disturbance to below-ground archaeology. Air-source heat pumps result in less disruption but are more visually intrusive and are potentially noisy. At Astley Castle, where they are linked to an underfloor heating system, the relatively large units are discreetly located beside one of the ruined walls to the side of the property and stand within a timber enclosure.

FLOODING

In improving the resilience of buildings to flooding, a balance has to be struck between intervention and maintaining historic character. Existing rainwater and drainage systems should be upgraded wherever possible so they are capable of

Figure 7.27
PV panels and rooflights at the Old Railway Quarter, Swindon.

Figure 7.28
Air-source heat pump units concealed at Astley Castle, Warwickshire (right).

Figure 7.29
Flood-proof external shutters on an Edinburgh building. (far right)

removing excess water efficiently in extreme weather events. These might be complemented by SuDS (sustainable drainage systems), which are designed to mimic nature and typically manage rainfall close to source. Flood barriers, gates or doors may be installed and landscaping undertaken to create bunds. To aid drying out in the event of a flood, buildings constructed using breathable materials must be allowed to breathe, so waterproof membranes, sealants and cement-based products should be avoided. Lime-based plasters soften when wet but harden again when dry, whereas modern gypsum-based plasters deteriorate when wet and have to be removed.

Key design measures to lessen the impact of flooding include:

» provision of temporary covers to service points and air vents, particularly those venting under suspended timber floors

» electrical intakes and mains panels installed on upper floors

» electrical outlets and switches positioned above potential flood levels with cables run down from ceilings (chasing of walls should be minimised or avoided where damage may be done to historic fabric)

» non-return valves fitted to drainage systems to prevent foul water entering the building

» breathable limecrete used instead of concrete for floors

» free-standing furniture in kitchens and other ground-floor areas, rather than fitted units.

MAINTENANCE

The importance of ongoing, preventive maintenance of buildings of all types cannot be overstated and is a key precept of the SPAB Manifesto, which calls upon those who have to deal with buildings to 'stave off decay by daily care'. Maintenance forestalls as well as cures problems and so is the most practical and economic form of conservation and is vital to the sustainability of buildings. Effective maintenance will minimise problems, for example, from blocked and overflowing rainwater goods which cause walls to become damp. From an energy performance perspective, damp walls are cold walls, which results in higher levels of heating to avoid an uncomfortable and unhealthy internal environment. All buildings – old and new – should have a plan that ensures regular checks are made on all key areas and that any need for remediation is identified and resulting work is carried out promptly and efficiently. Known maintenance needs, including decorating, are best scheduled at regular intervals, with gutters and gullies cleared at least annually in the autumn. This work should be geared to minimising damage to the building's fabric as well as any waste of resources, energy and money.

To emphasise the importance of regular maintenance and encourage it for buildings of all types and ages, the SPAB founded an annual event, National Maintenance Week, which is now widely supported by communities and local councils across the UK. In the case of churches, the SPAB has a long history of supporting and training church staff and volunteers through its Faith in Maintenance programme and Maintenance Cooperative Project.

Figure 7.30
A gutter and parapet requiring maintenance.

FUTURE-PROOFING

The loose-fit nature of many old buildings has been essential to their successful adaptation and re-use. Future adaptability and flexibility should always enter the debate when designing new spaces or buildings, and the priority must be to find the best possible solution rather than creating a compromise or generic building. It is important to future-proof the design as far as possible so that new work will not need to be revisited for many decades.

Many considerations and factors are essential to achieving this. A deep understanding and respect for the building that is being adapted will deliver the best outcomes. Detailing and specification play a key role, with high-quality materials and craftsmanship making for comfortable, attractive and, most importantly, enduring buildings where a successful new body of architecture is created through the sum of new and old parts.

Figure 7.31
Hunsett Mill in Norfolk, where a deep understanding of the old has led to the successful creation of the new.